W9-CBF-753

3 3013 00123742 3

BRADNER LIBRARY
SCHOOLCRAFT COLLEGE
18600 HAGGERTY ROAD
LIVONIA, MICHIGAN 48152

WITHDRAWN

E 332 .H66 2005b
Hitchens, Christopher.
Thomas Jefferson

Thomas Jefferson

Eminent Lives, brief biographies by distinguished authors on canonical figures, joins a long tradition in this lively form, from Plutarch's *Lives* to Vasari's *Lives of the Painters*, Dr. Johnson's *Lives of the Poets* to Lytton Strachey's *Eminent Victorians*. Pairing great subjects with writers known for their strong sensibilities and sharp, lively points of view, the Eminent Lives are ideal introductions designed to appeal to the general reader, the student, and the scholar. "To preserve a becoming brevity which excludes everything that is redundant and nothing that is significant," wrote Strachey: "That, surely, is the first duty of the biographer."

GENERAL EDITOR: JAMES ATLAS

ALSO BY CHRISTOPHER HITCHENS

Love, Poverty and War: Journeys and Essays
A Long Short War: The Postponed Liberation of Iraq
Blood, Class, and Empire:
The Enduring Anglo-American Relationship
For the Sake of Argument: Essays and Minority Reports
Hostage to History: Cyprus from the Ottomans to Kissinger
Letters to a Young Contrarian
Missionary Position: Mother Teresa in Theory and Practice
No One Left to Lie To: The Values of the Worst Family
The Trial of Henry Kissinger
Unacknowledged Legislation: Writers in the Public Sphere
Why Orwell Matters
Prepared for the Worst: Essays & Minority Reports
The Elgin Marbles
Blaming the Victims
(edited with Edward Said)

THOMAS JEFFERSON

Author of America

Christopher Hitchens

EMINENT LIVES

ATLAS
BOOKS

HarperCollins*Publishers*

E
332
.H66
2005b

Grateful acknowledgment is made for permission to reprint from the
following: "New Year Letter." Copyright © 1941 by W. H. Auden.
Reprinted by permission of Curtis Brown, Ltd.

THOMAS JEFFERSON. Copyright © 2005 by Christopher Hitchens. All
rights reserved. Printed in the United States of America. No part of
this book may be used or reproduced in any manner whatsoever without written permission except in the case of brief quotations embodied in critical articles and reviews. For information, address
HarperCollins Publishers, 10 East 53rd Street, New York, NY 10022.

HarperCollins books may be purchased for educational, business, or
sales promotional use. For information, please write: Special Markets
Department, HarperCollins Publishers, 10 East 53rd Street, New
York, NY 10022.

FIRST EDITION

Designed by Elliott Beard

Printed on acid-free paper

Library of Congress Cataloging-in-Publication Data is available
upon request.

ISBN 0-06-059896-4

05 06 07 08 09 ❖/RRD 10 9 8 7 6 5 4 3

For Brian Lamb: a great Virginian and a great American,
a fine democrat as well as a good republican,
who has striven for an educated electorate

Contents

Acknowledgments

MY PRINCIPAL THANKS are due to the late William Apple-
ton Coolidge of Topsfield, Massachusetts. A direct descendant of Ellen Wayles Coolidge, Thomas Jefferson's granddaughter by
Thomas Mann and Martha Jefferson Randolph, he endowed the
Atlantic Crossing scholarship at Balliol College, Oxford, which first
brought me to these United States in 1970 and which makes me, I
suppose, an indirect beneficiary of the peculiar Monticello system.

In January and February of 2004, I was invited to give four lec-
tures and two seminars on Thomas Jefferson at the James Madison
College of Michigan State University. The LeFrak Forum and Sym-
posium on Science, Reason, and Modern Democracy provided me
with an environment that was at once welcoming and intimidating,
and I want very warmly to thank its directors, Arthur Melzer, Jerry
Weinberger, and Richard Zinman, for giving me the opportunity of
testing my opinions and conclusions against those of superior mind
and experience.

Acknowledgments

It was a fair wind that brought me, some years ago, into contact with Professor Annette Gordon Reed of New York University. Her pursuit of truth in the study of Jefferson is a model of historical objectivity, forensic scruple, and moral sense.

To have decided to pass a certain time "immersed" either in Jefferson's work or in works about Jefferson is as impossible to regret as it is near impossible to undertake. No single person can now claim to have the entire store of existing knowledge. Everybody concerned must, of course, dip their flags to Julian Boyd, editor of the still-expanding twenty-seven-volume edition of *The Papers of Thomas Jefferson* prepared for the press at Princeton University, and to Dumas Malone's six-volume biography *Jefferson and His Time*. It is an honor, even when it is not a pleasure, to register disagreement with the second of these. The finest, and the best written, of the more condensed Jefferson biographies is Merrill Peterson's, succeeded, as I am sure he would himself admit, by the work of R. B. Bernstein.

Gore Vidal's *Burr* is the best fictional re-creation of the period and forms a keystone in the grand historical-novelistic architecture that is already Mr. Vidal's memorial. Conor Cruise O'Brien's *The Long Affair* is the most eloquent of the anti-Jeffersonian nonfictions, followed by the work of Albert Jay Nock. John Chester Miller's *The Wolf by the Ears* was for me the most various and illuminating account of the slavery question. On the much-neglected subject of the Barbary war, I found myself gratefully dependent upon *Jefferson's War*, by Joseph Whelan, and upon *To the Shores of Tripoli*, by A. B. C.

Whipple, upon Evan Thomas's *John Paul Jones*, and even more dependent on Linda Colley's *Captives*, which reminded me once again that much of the Jeffersonian story is to be found in books that are ostensibly concerned with other subjects. This would also be true of *Undaunted Courage*, Stephen Ambrose's account of the Lewis and Clark expedition, of John Keane's exceptional biography of Thomas Paine, of Ron Chernow's exemplary life of Alexander Hamilton, of Gordon S. Wood's *The Radicalism of the American Revolution*, Bernard Bailyn's *Ideological Origins of the American Revolution*, and of Theodore Draper's astonishingly original account of the American Revolution, *A Struggle for Power*, which replaces that emphasis on radicalism in another way. Those who study Jefferson must also study Edmund Burke, an obvious admission which again puts me in the debt of Conor Cruise O'Brien for his book *The Great Melody* and of David Bromwich for his meticulous editing of Burke's writings *On Empire, Liberty, and Reform*.

Jefferson's Children: The Story of One American Family, by Shannon Lanier and Jane Feldman, is one of the most striking pieces of Americana ever published. It assembles all the living descendants of Thomas Jefferson and Sally Hemings, and prints their photographs as well as their narratives. The book carries an introduction by Lucian K. Truscott IV, an "authorized" direct descendant of Jefferson—his fifth great-grandson—whose decency and honesty helped bring about this reunion, and who thereby helped refute his ancestor's sorry belief that such love, coexistence, and mutual esteem would never be possible. *Mutato nomine, et de te fabula narratur.*

To list more sources might be to run the risk of boasting rather than acknowledging. I have learned in the course of this undertaking that anyone who writes about America is writing about Thomas Jefferson in one way or another, and so—as with the magnificent Jefferson Room in the Library of Congress, where I have spent so many absorbing days in the last quarter-century—I am tempted to annex, with all their ambivalence, the incised lines that commemorate Sir Christopher Wren at St. Paul's: Reader, if you seek his monument, look around you.

Thomas Jefferson

Introduction

To BEGIN, THEN, at the conclusion. On June 24, 1826, Thomas Jefferson wrote his last letter. Addressed from his Virginia home, Monticello, it was sent in response to an invitation from Roger C. Weightman, the chairman of a Washington committee to celebrate the then-impending fiftieth anniversary of the Declaration of Independence. Jefferson proffered regrets that his fast-declining health would prevent him from making the journey to the capital. He went on to elaborate this regret in the following manner:

> I should, indeed, with peculiar delight, have met and ex-
> changed there congratulations personally with the small
> band, the remnant of that host of worthies who joined with
> us on that day, in the bold and doubtful election we were to
> make for our country, between submission or the sword; and
> to have enjoyed with them the consolatory fact, that our

fellow citizens, after half a century of experience and prosperity, continue to approve the choice we made. May it be to the world, what I believe it will be (to some parts sooner, to others later, but finally to all), the signal of arousing men to burst the chains under which monkish ignorance and superstition had persuaded them to bind themselves, and to assume the blessings and security of self-government. That form which we have substituted, restores the free right to the unbounded exercise of reason and freedom of opinion. All eyes are opened, or opening, to the rights of man. The general spread of the light of science has already laid open to every view the palpable truth, that the mass of mankind has not been born with saddles on their backs, nor a favored few booted and spurred, ready to ride them legitimately, by the grace of God. These are grounds of hope for others. For ourselves, let the annual return of this day forever refresh our recollections of these rights, and an undiminished devotion to them.

Thomas Jefferson died on the immediately following Fourth of July, killed by a wasting diarrhea and an infection of the urinary tract. His final words were: "Is it the Fourth?" On the same day, his great rival John Adams died at Quincy, Massachusetts. His final words were: "Thomas Jefferson still lives," or, at the very least, "Thomas Jefferson . . ." Many tales of the last words of famous men are apocryphal, or are pious fabrications, but these seem tolerably well authenticated.

In the above letter, Jefferson touched upon all the chief points of his political life. He did not need to mention his own authorship of the Declaration, the preamble to which had established the concept of human rights, for the first time in history, as the basis for a republic. He trenchantly restated the view that the American Revolution was founded on universal principles, and was thus emphatically for export. He laid renewed stress on the importance of science and innovation as the spur of the Enlightenment, and scornfully contrasted this with mere faith and credulity. His open skepticism in point of religion is the more striking given that he had by that date already made his own will, designed his own tombstone, and told his physicians that he was quite prepared for death.

There are only two biographical essays that enable an author to consider and reconsider the whole idea of the United States *ab initio*, and these are the lives of Thomas Jefferson and Abraham Lincoln. Seventeen at the time of Jefferson's death, and dividing his time between axmanship and plying the oars of a ferry, Lincoln was later to say, in 1859:

All honor to Jefferson: to the man who, in the concrete pressure of a struggle for national independence by a single people, had the coolness, forecast and capacity to introduce into a merely revolutionary document an abstract truth, applicable to all men and all times, and so to embalm it there, that today, and in all coming days, it shall be a rebuke and a stumbling-block to the very harbingers of reappearing tyranny and oppression.

When Lincoln later came to ponder, in his address at Gettysburg, whether the American ideal could long endure, it was to Jefferson's Declaration of Independence ("four score and seven years" before 1863) and not to the federal Constitution that he applied his moral attention. And this was most generous of him. If one now glances approvingly at those sentences in Jefferson's closing message that denounce the notion of some humans being born with saddles and other humans with spurs, one also knows that Jefferson himself need only have looked out of his own windows to see hereditary servitude in active operation. He deliberately postponed any reckoning with this evil, and consciously deeded it as part of his legacy to future generations. One score and seventeen years after Jefferson's own death, the killed and wounded at Gettysburg (an engagement that took place on the eve of the Fourth of July) set a new standard for horror in modern warfare.

Yet if it were not for Jefferson's exertions, there would have been no grand Union, even if it was "half-slave and half-free," for Lincoln and Douglas, and later Lincoln and Davis, and ultimately Grant and Lee, to contest. It was on the Fourth of July, 1803, that the *National Intelligencer* of Washington printed the news of the Louisiana Purchase, perhaps the greatest land deal in history, whereby Napoleon Bonaparte agreed to sell everything between the Mississippi River and the Rocky Mountains—a tranche of land then uncharted in respect of its full northern extent—to the United States. This transaction, which was the result of careful secret diplomacy and some deft short-circuiting of Congress and the Constitution, did not so much enlarge the United States as actually transform it: at any rate doubling its existing land area at a cost of four cents an acre. Later on the same day, Colonel Merriwether Lewis received his final letter of credit from President Jefferson and made ready to embark upon the most ambitious adventure of Enlightenment exploration that had ever been conceived, let alone attempted. The Fourth of July, 1803, deserves a higher place than it normally receives in the list of hinge events or crucial dates in the human story. But it was not a date on which anything actually happened. Rather, it was a day when one careful scheme was consummated and another inaugurated. Modern and postmodern historians are fond of using terms such as "inventing America" or "imagining America." It would be truer to say, of Thomas Jefferson, that he *designed* America, or that he authored it.

This being the case, it would be lazy or obvious to say that he contained contradictions or paradoxes. This is true of everybody, and of everything. It would be infinitely more surprising to strike upon a historic figure, or indeed a nation, that was *not* subject to this law. Jefferson did not embody contradiction. Jefferson *was* a contradiction, and this will be found at every step of the narrative that goes to make up his life.

Chapter One

All Politics Is Local:
Virginia to Philadelphia

B ORN ON APRIL 13, 1743 (April 2 until the adoption of the Gregorian calendar in 1758), Thomas Jefferson was the offspring of stable planter stock in the native aristocracy of Virginia. His father, Peter Jefferson, was a surveyor and cartographer whose immigrant parents were said to have come from the Snowdonia district of northern Wales. Peter's marriage to Jane Randolph, whose own family was one of the "names" of traditional Virginia society, can only have improved his standing. Perhaps it was young Jefferson's evident contempt and dislike for his mother—to whom he almost never alluded—or his apparent indifference to aristocracy, but when he came to write his own very brief *Autobiography* in 1821, he spoke of these matters of bloodline and provenance and "pedigree," especially in his mother's case, with an affected indifference. "Let everyone," he wrote, "ascribe the faith and merit he chooses," to such trifling questions. Since Jefferson always founded American claims of right upon the ancient Saxon autonomy supposedly established by the near-mythical English kings Hengist and Horsa, who had left Saxony and established a form of self-rule in southern England (he even wished to see their imagined likeness on the first Great Seal of the United States), we are confronted at once with his fondness for, if not indeed his need for, the negation of one of his positions by another.

We cannot hope to peer very far past the opaque curtain that is always in evidence (and also not in evidence) when a young man seemingly reveres his father and is indifferent to his mother. However, the nature of individual humans is not radically different and it's no great surprise to discover that the adolescent Thomas felt himself liable at one point to go to seed and to waste his time on loose company. We find, also, an excruciating account of a "bad date" at the Apollo Room of the Raleigh Tavern when, nerving himself to make advances to the much sought-after Rebecca Burwell, he made an utter hash of the approach and a more or less complete fool of himself. ("Good God!" he wrote to a friend the following morning. Later, news that Miss Burwell—the sister of a classmate and the daughter of a family estate in York County—was betrothed to another man was to give young Thomas the first of the many migraine attacks that plagued him intermittently through life.) That this initial reverse was a sting is not to be doubted. Nor is it to be doubted that it was followed by still another fiasco, when he made a crass and unsuccessful attempt to seduce the wife of his friend John Walker. I mention this because it demonstrates that Jefferson was ardent by nature when it came to females, and also made reticent and cautious by experience. This is worth knowing from the start, and would scarcely need to be observed at all if it were not for the generations of historians who have written, until the present day, as if he were not a male mammal at all.

He recovered from his early instability in three principal ways: by adopting the study of the classics, by pursuing the practice of law, and by making an excellent marriage. These avenues converged on a single spot, still revered by Americans and also made part of the small change of their experience by featuring in image on the reverse of the humble nickel, or five-cent coin. A Palladian house named Monticello, on a mountaintop in the Virginia wilderness (and built with its front facing the untamed West), emerged as the centerpiece of a life which could well, were it not for some accidents of history, have been devoted to uxoriousness, agricultural husbandry, hunting, bibliophilia, and the ingenious prolongation of chattel slavery.

The difference was made by Jefferson's attendance, between 1760 and 1762, at William and Mary College in Williamsburg. Here, he had the best luck that a young man can have, in that he was fortunate with his tutors. In particular, he fell in with Dr. William Small, a Scots-born teacher of the scientific method, and with the great George Wythe, who taught the law as an aspect of history and logic and humanism and who seems to have adopted the young man as a personal protégé. Once aroused, the thirst for learning was unslakeable in Jefferson for the rest of his life; as unappeasable, in fact, as his longing for the possession of books and the acquisition of their contents. Among the authors whose work he assimilated at this time was Lord Bolingbroke, a pioneer critic of organized Christianity. For anyone even reasonably attuned, the air was full of Enlightenment thinking at the time, and blowing from England and Scotland as well as from France. (It was to waft Thomas Paine across the Atlantic, among other things, bearing a letter of introduction from the learned Dr. Benjamin Franklin.) Private in this as in so many things, Jefferson never made any ostentatious renunciation of religion, but his early detachment from its mystical or "revealed" elements was to manifest itself throughout his mature life.

To have a proper photograph of Shakespeare, Susan Sontag once wrote, would be the modern equivalent of possessing a splinter from the True Cross. We naturally do not possess a photograph of Thomas Jefferson, but we have a number of portraits of him at numerous stages of his life, and a wealth of eyewitness descriptions. By the time he came to Williamsburg, he was very tall for his age and indeed very tall for his times, standing two inches above six feet. He was neither clumsy nor particularly graceful, having long but somewhat loose limbs. Reddish of hair and freckled of complexion, he possessed hazel eyes, thin lips, and a rather prominent nose and chin. If one plays the parlor game—"If he were to be an animal, which animal would he be?"—we are almost compelled to think of a large and rather resourceful fox.

The exigencies of family and position required a good marriage of this vulpine fellow, and Jefferson made one in 1772 with Martha Wayles Skelton, who was five years his junior. She became the mistress of Monticello, sharing her husband's fondness for music (he had learned the violin at the age of nine). An ominous note intrudes itself here: a few months before his wedding he had written to one of his in-laws, Robert Skipwith, recommending Locke, Montesquieu, Hume, and other authors of the Enlightenment to him but also strongly approving Lawrence Sterne. This endorsement occurs even more forcefully in a 1787 letter to his cousin Peter Carr, where Jefferson describes Sterne's work as "the best course of morality that ever was written." We know, furthermore, that Thomas and Martha took an early mutual delight in Sterne's *Tristram Shandy,* even reading it aloud to one another during those long evenings. We must thus, from the first, appreciate what becomes ever clearer as the story proceeds: we are studying a man with very little sense of humor.

As the young Jefferson was growing to manhood and acquiring the habits and lineaments of an educated gentleman, a historic power struggle was developing on the northern border of British North America. The Seven Years' War between Britain and France, known in American history books as the French and Indian War, prefigured the later Napoleonic conflict by fighting itself out on several continents. British and French forces clashed in Europe, on the high seas, and in India and the Caribbean. Employing local tribes as surrogates and proxies, they also fought bitterly over Canada and especially Quebec. General James Wolfe's capture of the latter in late 1759 can well be described as a turning point in history: it decided that the future world language would be English and it indirectly precipitated the American Revolution, which in turn caused the British Empire to establish Australia as an alternative destination for convicts and malcontent laborers.

In London, an immense argument broke out concerning the future of victorious British policy. The Indian sub-continent had been wrested from France for good: the eventual Treaty of Paris in 1763 would allow Britain to take command of at least one more French possession. The choices narrowed themselves to two: Guadeloupe or Canada. One faction urged the claims of Guadeloupe, an island rich in sugar and spices and slaves, the addition of which would almost complete British control of the Caribbean basin. Another party spoke up for the acquisition of Canada: a vast space for settlement, potentially abundant in furs and timber and minerals, and a grand future market for British manufactured goods. The second case—more forward-looking and commercial—seemed in many respects the stronger and more persuasive one. It did, however, contain an overlooked flaw. If the British Crown took possession of Canada, the thirteen American colonies would no longer need to depend on London's military protection against France. Once out from under that "umbrella," what thoughts of self-determination might start to infiltrate their consciousness? This argument was made, with considerable force, in a pamphlet by William Burke (a close colleague, but not a kinsman, of the more celebrated Edmund). He wrote:

> If, Sir, the People of our Colonies find no check from Canada, they will extend themselves, almost, without bounds

into the Inland Parts. They are invited into it by the Pleasantness, the Fertility, and the Plenty of that Country; and they will increase infinitely from all Causes. What the Consequence will be, to have a numerous, hardy, independent People, possessed of a strong Country, communicating little or not at all with England, I leave to your own reflections. I hope we have not gone to these immense expenses, without any Idea of securing the Fruits of them to Posterity. If we have, I am sure we have acted with little Frugality, or Foresight.

William Burke was unusually prescient. The British did take Canada. They also decided to recoup the heavy expenses of the Seven Years' War, which had partly been fought to protect the thirteen colonies, by raising taxes on their supposedly grateful American subjects. This provoked a rebellion and ultimately a political separation in 1776, in which the military balance was tipped against Britain by a France that sought revenge for the humiliation of 1763. And the cost of this expedition to the depleted French treasury, in the opinion of many historians, precipitated the crisis of insolvency that compelled King Louis to summon the Estates General and begin the unraveling of the *ancien régime* that culminated in the revolution of 1789.

Thus, almost all of Jefferson's long political life is foreshadowed in Burke's analysis. An independent America was achievable, first by means of a skillful manipulation of the rivalries between the two former principal colonial powers, France and Britain, and second by playing a long hand with the ramshackle empire that had first conquered the Americas: the once-magnificent but now fast-declining Spain. Yet it could not be forgotten that America had less than five million inhabitants (nearly one-fifth of them African slaves) while France had twenty-seven million and Britain perhaps fifteen million people. Thus, the young republic had always to look to the vast interior on the edge of which it was so tenuously established. Within this quadrilateral of forces, Jefferson was to emerge as the republican equivalent of a philosopher king, who was coldly willing to sacrifice all principles and all allegiances to the one great aim of making America permanent.

It took some little time before Jefferson's own life became caught up to the same pace and rhythm as these parallel events were to dictate. In 1768, at the age of twenty-five, he had become a member of Virginia's House of Burgesses: a part-time local parliament made up largely of his own class, and without much fatiguing exertion about the matter of election. Nonetheless, Jefferson took his duties with seriousness and embarked—in the literal sense—upon a project that seems to show how early the pattern of his life was set. He set off in a canoe to discover the reasons why the Rivanna River could not be open to navigation. Later listing the obstacles and finding them superable, he initiated a plan for the clearing of the waterway and thus reduced the onerousness with which tobacco and other crops had hitherto been conveyed by land to the larger but more distant James River. This venture in practical science anticipates his later and grander dreams of a transcontinental "portage" by water, and his relentless concentration on the importance of the Mississippi. By 1773 he had become the Albermarle County surveyor—a profession in which George Washington had also distinguished himself—and may well have felt that, even if his father had held the same post, he had earned it in his own right.

That same year, his father-in-law John Wayles died. He left to his daughter (which in law at the time meant that he left to his son-in-law) an estate that doubled Jefferson's holding. He also bequeathed the slaves with whom to work the land, among them an illegitimate child of his—and thus Martha Jefferson's half sister—named Sally Hemings. The young Jefferson couple, meanwhile, were beginning to produce children of their own, of whom only two out of six were to outlive infancy. The acquisition of this new fortune in real estate and human property was, in radically different ways, to haunt Jefferson for the rest of his life, because it brought with it more debts and responsibilities than he was capable of managing. Still, at the time he could have congratulated himself on having a fine house, a growing family, the respect of his peers, and the chance of professional advancement.

In another epoch, he might have become locally famous as an autodidact and inventor, winning a bucolic reputation as a stern but kindly slave-master, and celebrated for the generosity of his table, the excellence of his wines, and the range of his library and conversation. But there was evidently something in him that caused impatience, and impelled him to seek a larger compass for his energy. Indeed, this was a time when the crisis of the British Empire in North America made it difficult for all but the most obtuse to be content with the merely private life.

In 1773, however, Jefferson was still able to keep an equilibrium between that private life and his public responsibilities. He was also able to imagine a balance—which proved to be illusory—between the political claims of Virginia in particular, the thirteen colonies in general, and the continuation of Crown rule in North America. A few dress rehearsals of rebellion had taken place: in May of 1769 the normally placid House of Burgesses in Virginia had been dissolved by the British governor in consequence of its insubordination in the matter of taxes, but the members, including Jefferson, strolled coolly down the street to the Apollo Room of the Raleigh Tavern—scene of his rejection on the dance floor by the maddening Miss Burwell—and there reconstituted themselves as an "Association" pledged to boycott goods taxed by Parliament. (A monograph should be written on the role of the tavern in the American Revolution.) This was all good sport by the standards of the day, and the rebellion politely fizzled out within a year. It remains noteworthy for our purposes, however, and for two reasons. The first of these is that the testy if dexterous governor, Norborne Berkeley, Baron de Botetourt, was by his name and title a perfect emblem of that "Norman yoke" on ancient English liberty which Paine, Jefferson, and many others were beginning to revive as an article of propaganda. The second is that the idea of economic warfare—of sanctions, boycotts, and embargoes—had taken root in Jefferson's receptive mind.

Tame as the Virginia House of Burgesses might be, at least when compared with what was to come, it did furnish Jefferson with the opportunity to hear some full-dress revolutionary oratory from Patrick Henry and to persuade himself that his own talent lay in the opposite direction. Never an accomplished speaker (this is to say the very least, if we rely on contemporary accounts), he discovered a talent for the careful drafting of bills and measures, for the fusion of legal with political arguments, and for the intelligible synthesis of complicated ideas. Allied to his voracious talent as a reader, these gifts caused him to be in constant request as the quarrel with King George III mounted to a crisis. Thus in 1773 he was a founding and useful member of Virginia's "Committee of Correspondence," a legal means of establishing contact between opposition forces in all the disparate colonies and the germ of the Continental Congress. The resolution to establish such a committee (which has an echo of the radical "London Corresponding Society" across the water) was written by Jefferson. The next year, after the British imposition of collective punishment on Boston, and the famous response the fate of the East India Company's ill-conceived plan to dump its tea—which was then dumped in revenge—he helped to propose a Virginia resolution for a day of solidarity with the people of Massachusetts. This resolution having been adopted, the new British governor Lord Dunmore dissolved the House of Burgesses again, and once more Jefferson and his companions walked down to the Raleigh Tavern to refresh themselves and reconvene. Later in 1774, he adopted the pen name of "Virginian" to compose *A Summary View of the Rights of*

British America. This polemical treatise was a morally and legally necessary exercise, a sort of "last chance" warning to King George that the patience of his colonial subjects was not inexhaustible. Reprinted as a pamphlet in London, it had considerable influence on the debate then proceeding at Westminster, and it's surely worthy of mention that Edmund Burke himself—then a lobbyist for the colony of New York—helped to prepare it for the press as part of his own efforts at conciliation.

A Summary View shows that Jefferson was a loss to the law and the bar, and that a client who wished for an attorney who could plead on either side of a case would have done well to engage him. Strangely, perhaps, for one who was shortly going to be celebrated for proclaiming universal principles, Jefferson grounded his fundamental case upon an essentially tribal appeal. The ancient Saxon settlers in England, he said, had voluntarily removed themselves from the European continent to an island. And the American settlers in North America had voluntarily removed themselves in turn from that island to another continent. Both had established self-ruling and autonomous communities. No loss of rights was involved in either instance: the inborn and inherent freedom of the Saxon could no more be forfeited to King George than it could have been given up to the preceding Saxons of Germany. Rather, any Englishman anywhere had the same rights as an Englishman in England itself. From there, it was easy to demonstrate that the King and Parliament judged identical people by different standards: restricting commerce, levying taxes, and extending the jurisdiction of remote courts only upon the American branch. In a sarcastic remark about the effect of this on the unjustly penalized citizens of Boston, Jefferson said that they were now given up "to ruin, by that *unseen hand* which governs the momentous affairs of this great empire." It was not until 1776 that Adam Smith published his *Wealth of Nations*, a defense of free enterprise which, incidentally, maintained that colonies were a waste of resources. Perhaps he had glimpsed a stray copy of *A Summary View* before proposing his "invisible hand"?

In Jefferson's argument, the traditional liberties of the original Saxons had not been abolished in consequence of their defeat by William the Conqueror at Hastings in 1066. Rather, the whole of subsequent English history had been a slow but inexorable battle to reaffirm those same rights. Kipling, the bard of Anglo-Saxondom, was later to phrase it like this in his 1911 poem "Norman and Saxon," where a dying Norman baron of the year 1100 gives some advice to his heir:

> *The Saxon is not like us Normans. His manners are not so*
> *   polite.*
> *But he never means anything serious till he talks about*
> *   justice and right.*
> *When he stands like an ox in the furrow with his sullen set*
> *   eyes on your own,*
> *And grumbles, "This isn't fair dealing," my son, leave the*
> *   Saxon alone.*

The landmarks of this antique struggle were the Magna Carta of 1215, the forcible suppression of the divine right of kings at the close of the English Civil War, and the growth of the power of Parliament.

British Tories might take refuge in the idea of an "unwritten" constitution and an informal separation of powers, but in his dry reference to the "unseen," Jefferson was beginning to formulate the future concept of a written guarantee of rights. He was also connecting himself to a radical political and literary tradition in England, extending through the folk-memory of the Peasant's Revolt of 1381, the battle to have the Bible translated into English by Wycliffe and Tyndale, and the antimonarchic poetry of John Milton—who had penned the mighty line "By the known rules of ancient liberty." The ideal exemplar of this very tradition of English republicanism and anticlericalism, the self-taught staymaker and sacked exciseman Thomas Paine, was at this precise moment engaging in the discussions with fellow exiles that would lead him to publish *Common Sense*: the most successful pamphlet in history and one that would be the catalyst for full-hearted independence as the talisman for new-minted American pride.

In 1774, however, Jefferson and most of his associates still thought it just and prudent to clarify their differences with the Crown, and to beseech the king to keep the Anglo-Saxon family together under one imperial roof. "America was not conquered by William the Norman, nor its lands surrendered to him or any of his successors." There is no doubt a tone of condescension in the way that Jefferson phrased this (and it certainly had the effect of enraging the king and his ministers at his damned impudence), but the offer he made was nonetheless a handsome one:

Let no act be passed by any one legislature, which may infringe on the rights and liberties of another. This is the important post in which fortune has placed you, holding the balance of a great, if a well-poised empire. This, Sire, is the advice of your great American council, on the observance of which may perhaps depend your felicity and future fame, and the preservation of that harmony which alone can continue, both to Great Britain and America, the reciprocal advantages of their connection. It is neither our wish nor our interest to separate from her.

This was almost the last time that the latter sentiment could be uttered with any simulacrum of sincerity. In a warning paragraph just before this one, Jefferson had taken note of the presence of large bodies of British troops on American soil, "not made up of the people here, nor raised by the authority of our laws." In context, this was an allusion to the Hanoverian or Hessian origin of many of the occupying soldiers. In his later recollection of the debates that preceded the Declaration of Independence, Jefferson was to mention one geopolitical consideration which bore directly upon this: "That the only misfortune [was] that we did not enter into alliance with France six months sooner, as, besides opening her ports for the vent of our last year's produce, she might have marched an army into Germany, and prevented the petty princes there, from selling their unhappy subjects to subdue us." He always kept in mind the international balance of forces, and often viewed with favor the outbreak of hostility between any two or three of the superintending global forces of the period.

Between 1774 and 1776, however, American patriots could only rely on their own right arms. There was much natural hesitation about making a breach with the mother country, but the mother country's arrogant king and his Tory ministers made the life of the waverer much simpler by detecting the obviously seditious elements in Jefferson's suave *Summary View*, and in other similar and related protests, and by acting as if a state of rebellion already existed. Local assemblies were dissolved, soldiers disembarked, and proclamations of "treason" made. Bitter skirmishes were fought, mainly in Massachusetts. Loyalist and monarchist gentlemen began to leave, either for Canada or for London. In January 1776 Paine's imperishable polemic was an instant best-seller. By the summer, a Congress was meeting in Philadelphia and the advocates of revolution held the moral advantage, as well as the practical one, in its deliberations. Pausing only briefly to attend to his unloved mother's obsequies, Jefferson made his way there.

His fame as a drafter of resolutions, as a writer of great explicatory force, and, for that matter, as a thoughtful compromiser had preceded him. Indeed, it was partly as a result of a compromise that Jefferson was appointed to the committee charged with drawing up the Declaration. The author of the resolutions calling upon the thirteen colonies to announce independence, to form a "confederation and perpetual union," and to seek overseas recognition and military alliances was Richard Henry Lee, himself a Virginian. But he was needed at home, and Congress needed a Virginian just as it needed some New Englanders and some delegates from the middle colonies. John Adams, Benjamin Franklin, Roger Sherman of Connecticut, and Robert Livingston of New York comprised the rest of the drafting group.

There is no other example in history, apart from the composition of the King James version of the Bible, in which great words and concepts have been fused into poetic prose by the banal processes of a committee. And, as with the extraordinary convocation of religious scholars that met at Hampton Court under the direction of Lancelot Andrewes in 1604, and with the later gathering of polymaths and revolutionaries at Philadelphia in 1776, the explanation lies partly in the simultaneous emergence, under the pressure of a commonly understood moment of crisis and transition, of like-minded philosophers and men of action. Modesty deserves its tribute here, too: a determination to do the best that could be commonly wrought was a great corrective to vanity. Thomas Jefferson's modesty was sometimes of the false kind. We have too many instances of him protesting, throughout his political ascent, that the honor is too great, the burden too heavy, the eminence too high. (Rather as the Speaker of the House of Commons is still ceremonially dragged to his chair on his inauguration, as if being compelled to assume his commanding role.) However, someone had to pull together a first draft, and we have it on the word of his longtime rival John Adams that Jefferson's reticence in the matter was on this occasion fairly swiftly overcome. He was generally thought to be the better writer and the finer advocate: one might wish to have seen a Franklin version—which might at least have contained one joke—but it was not to be.

Several years were to elapse before Jefferson was acknowledged as the author of the Declaration, or until the words themselves had so to speak "sunk in" and begun to resonate as they still do. So it is further evidence of his *amour propre*, as well as of his sense of history and rhetoric, that he always resented the changes that the Congress made to his original. These are reproduced, as parallel text, in his own *Autobiography*, and have been as exhaustively scrutinized as the intellectual sources on which Jefferson called when he repaired to a modest boarding house for seventeen days, with only a slave valet named Jupiter, brought from Monticello, at his disposal.

The most potent works, observes the oppressed and haunted Winston Smith in George Orwell's *Nineteen Eighty-Four*, when he's read the supposedly "secret" book of the forbidden opposition, are the ones that tell you what you already know. (And, in the "Dictionary of Newspeak" that closes that novel, a certain paragraph of prose is given as an example of something that could not be translated into "Newspeak" terms. The paragraph begins, "We hold these truths to be self-evident . . .") Jefferson and Paine had this in common in that year of revolution; they had the gift of pithily summarizing what was already understood, and then of moving an already mobilized audience to follow an inexorable logic. But they also had to overcome an insecurity and indecision that is difficult for us, employing retrospect, to comprehend. Let not, in such circumstances, the trumpet give off an uncertain sound. So, after a deceptively

THOMAS JEFFERSON

modest and courteous paragraph that assumes the duty of making a full explanation and of manifesting "decent respect," the very first sentence of the actual declaration roundly states that certain truths are—crucial words—*self-evident*.

This style—terse and pungent, yet fringed with elegance—allied the plain language of Thomas Paine to the loftier expositions of John Locke, from whose 1690 *Second Treatise on Civil Government* some of the argument derived. (It is of interest that Locke, who wrote of slavery that it was "so vile and miserable an Estate of Man . . . that 'tis hardly to be conceived that an Englishman, much less a Gentleman, should plead for it," was also the draftsman for an absolutist slaveholding "Fundamental Constitution" of the Carolinas in 1669.) Jefferson radicalized Locke by grounding human equality on the observable facts of nature and the common human condition. Having originally written that rights are derived "from that equal creation," he amended the thought to say that men were "endowed by their Creator with certain unalienable rights," thus perhaps attempting to forestall any conflict between Deists and Christians. And, where Locke had spoken of "life, liberty, and property" as being natural rights, Jefferson famously wrote "life, liberty, and the pursuit of happiness." We differ still on whether this means seeking happiness or rather happiness itself as a pursuit, but given the advantageous social position occupied by most of the delegates at Philadelphia, it is very striking indeed that either notion should have taken precedence over property. The clear need of the hour was for inspiration (and property rights were to be restored to their customary throne when the

Constitution came to be written), but "the pursuit of happiness" belongs to that limited group of lapidary phrases that has changed history, and it seems that the delegates realized this as soon as they heard it.

Thomas Jefferson, indeed, is one of the small handful of people to have his very name associated with a form of democracy. The word was not in common use at the time, and was not always employed positively in any case. (John Adams tended to say "democratical" when he meant unsound or subversive.) But the idea that government arose from the people and was not a gift to them or an imposition upon them, was perhaps the most radical element in the Declaration. Jefferson was later to compare government with clothing as "the badge of lost innocence," drawing from the myth of original nakedness and guilt in the Garden of Eden. Paine in his *Common Sense* had said, "Society is produced by our wants and government by our wickedness." As a compromise between government as a necessary evil—or an inevitable one—and in the course of a bill of complaint against a hereditary monarch, the Declaration proposed the idea of "the consent of the governed" and thus launched the experiment we call American, or sometimes Jeffersonian, democracy.

The remaining bulk of the Declaration consisted of an itemized indictment of King George III for his many depredations and trespasses. One paragraph in this bill of charges was of especial importance to Jefferson, and he was never to reconcile himself to having it struck out by his fellow committee members. It read as follows:

He [King George] has waged cruel war against human nature itself, violating its most sacred rights of life and liberty in the persons of a distant people who never offended him, captivating and carrying them into slavery in another hemisphere, or to incur miserable death in their transportation hither. This piratical warfare, the opprobrium of INFIDEL powers, is the warfare of the CHRISTIAN king of Great Britain. Determined to keep open a market where MEN should be bought and sold, he has prostituted his negative for suppressing every legislative attempt to prohibit or restrain this execrable commerce. And that this assemblage of horrors might want no fact of distinguished dye, he is now exciting those very people to rise in arms amongst us, and to purchase that liberty of which he has deprived them, by murdering the people on whom he also obtruded them: thus paying off former crimes committed against the LIBERTIES of one people, with crimes which he urges them to commit against the LIVES of another.

The passage is of unusual interest. It shows that Jefferson understood not just the horrors of chattel slavery on American soil, but also the hellish conditions of the Middle Passage between Africa and America, where so many lives were callously extinguished. It also shows, by its use of the word *obtruded*, that he knew how to appeal to a certain self-righteousness in his audience (how dare black men fight on the side of the British, as they often did?) and—looking further ahead—that he saw no future for free black people in America. The references to the "piratical" and the "infidel" demonstrate an early awareness of the Muslim slave racket being carried on by the so-called Barbary powers of Islamic North Africa: yet another crisis which was to play its role in Jefferson's subsequent career.

It is possible, at one level, to read the omitted passage and to grieve at the fact that America declared its independence without repudiating its "original sin." The stone that should have been laid at the corner was discarded by the builders, with consequences that still have the power to make the reader tremble. However, Jefferson was perhaps a little naive, as well as a little self-righteous, when he attributed the excision of the above paragraph to the influence of "Georgia and South Carolina, who had never attempted to restrain the importation of slaves, and who, on the contrary, still wished to continue it." He even conceded as much in an indirect reference—both these lines are taken from his 1821 *Autobiography*—where he allowed that "our northern brethren also, I believe, felt a little tender under these censures; for though their people had very few slaves themselves, yet they had been pretty considerable carriers of them to others."

That would have been putting it very mildly in 1776. And it would furthermore have been absurd, at that time or any other, to put the blame for the slave trade entirely on King George. The American interest in the business, and the profits from it, were much too widely distributed to justify that assertion. Moreover, the claim that the king was at fault in imposing the trade had scarcely been so salient in Jefferson's *Summary View*, which had been intended as the last attempt at a full statement of grievance as well as the last effort at reconciliation, so it would have seemed decidedly odd to insert it so boldly at this climactic stage.

Jefferson had a tendency to confuse the issue of monarchy with the matter of slavery, at least in retrospect. Again in the *Autobiography* he recalls his early days in the Virginia legislature after 1769, and says: "I made one effort in that body for the permission of the emancipation of slaves, which was rejected: and indeed, during the regal government, nothing liberal could expect success." The phrase "permission of the emancipation of slaves," high-sounding as it may be, meant no more in fact than a legal recognition of the right of individuals to "manumit," or liberate their "own" property. It is, even so, asking too much to expect us to believe that, absent the royal prerogative, a House of Burgesses composed largely of a club of tobacco farmers would willingly have bestowed liberty on their slaves. The member with whom Jefferson concerted this mild proposal, Richard Bland, was denounced as "an enemy of his country." (Not, you note, an enemy of his king.) One is impelled to the slight suspicion that the young man was breaking a moral lance in a battle he could be sure of losing. And one also—employing now a retrospective wisdom—may imagine that he disliked the "obtrusion"—his proposed term in the Declaration—of a black population into Virginia in the first place, and subconsciously sought to blame a distant authority for this alien presence, or serpent, in the American Eden.

Such a reciprocal effect, between the politics of Virginia and the ideals of the emergent United States, was to preoccupy Jefferson for many years to come. Having completed his work on the Declaration and seen its truncated form adopted, he remained in Philadelphia in spite of the distance from his new and growing family, already depleted by the death of one infant daughter, and did not shirk his part in the slower and more quotidian work of the Congress. As always, he was a man of practice as well as ideas and delighted in the composition of exhaustive reports. One of these still exerts its influence: Jefferson successfully recommended the adoption of the Spanish "dollar," with its decimal principle, as the most rational unit of American currency.

Friedrich Engels once referred to revolutionary force as the midwife by whose efforts the new society was born of the body of the old. Many modern revolutions have made nonsense of this proposition, destroying existing social relations but failing to create civil societies. In the American case, however, a working model of a real political system was latently present, or pregnant, within the form of the existing British one. A government, an economy, a Congress, and an army were all in place, at least embryonically, long before independence was actually achieved, or had even been declared. And this potential new country and system had ambitions well beyond its immediate self. American forces, under the command of Benedict Arnold and Aaron Burr among others, had been sent to conquer Canada as early as 1775. (Despite the fiasco of this northern campaign, Jefferson and others always tended to assume that the errant former British and French provinces in Quebec and Ontario would eventually become part of the union.) Indeed, one of the many paradoxical consequences of the American revolution was that it helped consolidate British and royal power elsewhere in North America. Whether viewed as a continuation of the Seven Years' or French and Indian War or not, this unsuccessful lunge to the north demonstrated that the new republic harbored continental and even imperial ambitions.

By September of 1776 Jefferson felt that his place was back in Virginia, where he already held a seat in the legislature. Resigning from Congress, therefore, he returned home and found himself again embroiled in a contest over first principles. His native state had adopted a Constitution of its own in his absence, a document which Jefferson felt it essential to challenge because of its many entrenched conservative features. We can form an idea of the importance he attached to this, because we know that in the month of his return to Williamsburg—October 1776—he received notice of his election by Congress to be a negotiator of a Treaty of Alliance between the United States and France. This would necessitate his departure for Paris, together with Benjamin Franklin and Silas Deane. He phrased his rejection in terms now familiar to us, speaking of his need to spend more time with his family. Nor was this a mere formula of etiquette: he and his wife had already lost one child in infancy, and now Martha herself was far from well. The house and estate of Monticello required attention. But Jefferson also wanted to prove himself in Virginia politics, which were now emancipated from royal control.

Chapter Two

War and Revolution in Virginia

THREE SALIENT QUESTIONS would demonstrate whether the American Revolution, at the Virginia level, was to be truly a change of system and not a change of master. These were land tenure, slavery, and the state maintenance of religion. Superimposed was the issue of who was to decide: the people or the traditional authorities.

Land reform was the first of these battles. Jefferson detested because of its Norman and anti-Saxon features, the local law that upheld entail and primogeniture or, to phrase it more simply, the code of English feudalism. This code meant that land could be held by families in perpetuity and that, in the case of an intestate landowner's death, his holding would pass entirely to his oldest son. After a long argument which included a tussle between his old teacher George Wythe and the more traditionalist Edmund Pendleton, the Jeffersonian side won the day and both entail and primogeniture were eventually, and after many delaying tactics in committee, abolished.

As for slavery, the best Jefferson could do was to introduce a bill that forbade the further importation of Africans into Virginia, hoping, as he put it, to stop "the increase of the evil" thereby and to leave "to future efforts its final eradication." (In those last words, one can hear the tramp of General Lee's Army of Northern Virginia.) Had Jefferson had his way, he was later to claim, all those born after a certain date would have been liberated—and then deported. As he stated baldly when recalling the bill in his *Autobiography*:

> Nothing is more certainly written in the book of fate, than that these people are to be free; nor is it less certain that the two races, equally free, cannot live in the same government. Nature, habit, opinion have drawn indelible lines of distinction between them.

Only the first eighteen words of this passage are incised in stone on the Jefferson Memorial in Washington, D.C., which was dedicated by Franklin Roosevelt, in a moment of optimism about human rights, on Jefferson's bicentennial in April 1943.

The passage actually becomes more explicit as it goes on, warning that if emancipation and expatriation were not achieved peacefully, the same outcomes would be compelled by war, and that "human nature must shudder at the prospect held up. We should in vain look for an example in the Spanish deportation *or deletion* of the

Moors. This precedent would fall far short of our case." It conveys some idea of the morbid guilt and horror with which slaveholders viewed the possibility of black revenge that their most enlightened spokesman could compare his chattels with a medieval Islamic army. And I scarcely need to italicize the word *deletion* above, except for the fact that this sanguinary euphemism is generally omitted from the record. In the result, during Jefferson's time in Virginia politics the importation of slaves was ended and it was made easier for masters to free, or manumit, them. The temptation to do this was one that Jefferson himself resisted, except in the case of the children he fathered with Sally Hemings.

Two other areas of the law allowed more scope for Jefferson's Enlightenment convictions. The most conspicuous of these concerned religious liberty. Since its foundation, Virginia had maintained an established Episcopal Church, on the model of the Church of England. This meant that all the inhabitants of the colony were obliged to pay for the upkeep of this one clerical authority, an authority which in its turn demanded not only a confessional monopoly but the right to punish non-Anglican believers such as Baptists and Quakers. Resentment of the rich lands claimed by the Episcopalian bishops and ministers, combined with the hostility generated by the church's support for the king, might have made it seem easy to press for dis-Establishment after 1776. However, Jefferson meant to go further than that, and to legislate for a complete separation—he was later to call it a "wall"—between religion and the state. The matter proceeded by degrees, with a gradual repeal of those laws that penalized any religious opinions or practices (or any abstention from religious observance) and of the law that compelled "dissenters" to pay for the upkeep of the established church. A majority in the legislature was still Episcopalian, and each measure was very hard fought. None more so than Jefferson's proposed bill for establishing religious freedom, which was first presented in 1779. Its preamble stated:

> Well aware that Almighty God hath created the mind free; that all attempts to influence it by temporal punishments or burdens, or by civil incapacitations, tend only to beget habits of hypocrisy and meanness, and are a departure from the plan of the Holy Author of our religion, who being Lord both of body and mind, yet chose not to propagate it by coercions on either, as was in his Almighty power to do; that the impious presumption of legislators and rulers, civil as well as ecclesiastical, who, being themselves but fallible and uninspired men have assumed dominion over the faith of others, setting up their own opinions and modes of thinking as the only true and infallible, and as such endeavoring to impose them on others, hath established and maintained false religions over the greater part of the world and through all time.

Jefferson went on to say that "our civil rights have no dependence on our religious opinions, more than our opinions in physics or geometry" and that religious tests for public office constituted no more than "bribing, with a monopoly of worldly honors and emoluments, those who will externally profess and conform to it; that though indeed these are criminal who do not withstand such temptation, yet neither are those innocent who lay the bait in their way."

There was a small element of hypocrisy in Jefferson's own position, since as a "Deist" he did not believe that God intervened in human affairs at all, and was thus in a weak position to claim divine authority for a secular bill. He also argued for and against himself at the close of the bill, where it is stated that while of course no future Virginia assembly can be prevented from repealing the law, such a repeal would nonetheless be "an infringement of natural right." (Jefferson otherwise always maintained that rights belonged only to the living.) However, he was in a better logical and moral position than his rival Patrick Henry, who proposed an almost polytheistic alternative whereby not one, but *all* of the Christian churches be supported by the taxpayer. Here, Jefferson's great friend and ally James Madison was ready with a "Memorial and Remonstrance Against Religious Assessments":

Who does not see that the same authority which can establish Christianity, in exclusion of all other religions, may establish with the same ease any particular set of Christians, in exclusion of all other sects? That the same authority which can force a citizen to contribute three pence only of his property for the support of any one establishment, may force him to conform to any other establishment in all cases whatsoever? . . . What influence have ecclesiastical establishments had on Civil Society? In some instances they have been seen to erect a spiritual tyranny on the ruins of Civil authority; in many instances they have seen the upholding of the thrones of political tyranny; in no instance have they been seen the guardians of the liberty of the people. Rulers who wish to subvert the public liberty, may have found an established clergy convenient auxiliaries. A just government, instituted to secure and perpetuate liberty, needs them not.

When the Jefferson-Madison arguments eventually carried the day, the opposing side attempted even so to amend the preamble and to replace the words *Almighty God* in the first line with the words *Jesus Christ.* The defeat of this amendment, by a substantial majority, was cited by Jefferson as "proof that they meant to comprehend, within the mantle of its protection, the Jew and the Gentile, the Christian and Mahomedan, the Hindoo, and Infidel of every denomination." Until 1776, the common-law punishment for "heresy" in Virginia had been burning.

The Virginia Statute was passed only one year before the Constitutional Convention in Philadelphia, and greatly influenced the omission of any mention of God from the resulting document, as well as the stipulation in Article 6, Section 3, that "no religious test" be required for the holding of any office. There were many contrasting precedents on which the Framers might have drawn, though by definition they could not have employed all of them. The Massachusetts Constitution of 1780 extended equal protection, and the right to hold office, only to Christians and only to those Christians who abjured the pope. The New York Constitution of 1777 allowed equality to Jews but not to Catholics. In Maryland the situation was almost the reverse, with rights for Catholics and Protestants but not for Jews, Deists, and freethinkers. Delaware required its officeholders to swear to a belief in the Trinity, while South Carolina established "Protestantism" as its official religion. Virginia was the largest state in the new Union, and because of the presence of so many of its sons in the events of 1776 it had considerable revolutionary prestige as well as weight. It is not entirely fanciful to propose that its Statute on Religious Freedom was seminal in the "establishment" clause of the First Amendment.

The second area in which Jefferson deployed Enlightenment philosophy as a means of policy was that of crime and punishment. Like many of his educated contemporaries, he had been influenced by Cesare Beccaria's *Dei delitti e delle pene* (On Crimes and Punishments) published in Milan in 1764, and had copied no less than twenty-six extracts of it into his 1776 *Commonplace Book*. John Adams had quoted from Beccaria in his celebrated defense of the British soldiers unjustly accused during the Boston Massacre. Benjamin Franklin admired Beccaria hugely. Indeed, one of the great reproaches of the eighteenth-century radicals and liberals against the hereditary despotisms of the day was the lavish use that monarchy made of torture and of capital punishment. Beccaria's treatise had exposed the futility and stupidity, as well as the sadism, of these practices—condemned as "cruel and unusual" in the language of the Eighth Amendment to the federal Constitution.

Jefferson in 1778 proposed a "Bill of Proportion in Crimes and Punishments" to the Virginia House of Delegates. Beccaria, he wrote, "had satisfied the reasonable world of the unrightfulness and inefficiency of the punishment of crimes by death." As a substitute, he put forward a scheme of hard labor on public works. The measure was rejected by one vote, though it passed in a diluted form in 1796. Even though he was too ready to accept the inhuman practice of solitary confinement, which was later to be refined from Beccaria in the penal system proposed by Jeremy Bentham, Jefferson continued to press for a distinction between murder and manslaughter, which was recast as murder in the first and second degree, and to evolve his interest in the notion of the "penitentiary" as a scientific matter, with graduated and appropriate punishments. Again, none of this careful, measured liberalism was to be extended to those of African descent.

Jefferson was thirty-six when he became Virginia's second governor, succeeding Patrick Henry—who had completed his allotted maximum of three consecutive terms—in 1779. The election was a rather amicable and gentlemanly affair, decided by Virginia's General Assembly, and it gave Jefferson a slight margin over his friend John Page. Jefferson would probably have been happiest designing a new state capital in Richmond, and giving himself scope for his architectural leanings, but the state was still at war with the king of Great Britain and this brute fact dominated his tenure in office. The capital was in fact moved to Richmond from Williamsburg, as Jefferson had wished, but only because it was farther from the sea and thus less vulnerable to British attack. (Not much less vulnerable, as Benedict Arnold was to prove when he briefly seized the city in 1781.) Lord Cornwallis's redcoats entered Virginia, in strength sufficient to outmaneuver the dashing Marquis de Lafayette, and it was not long before Richmond in turn was given up by the Continental forces and the seat of government transferred to Charlottesville, Jefferson's hometown. His career, and possibly his life, could have ended right there if not for the southern version of Paul Revere's ride. A resourceful Virginia cavalryman named Jack Jouett observed a fast-moving column heading toward Monticello under the command of Lieutenant Colonel Banastre Tarleton, and spurred his horse into a forty-mile overnight dash to warn the Virginians that the British were coming, and coming swiftly. Jefferson was barely able to oversee the evacuation of the state government to the town of Staunton before the invader was at his own doorstep. A number of his slaves seized the chance to bolt—perhaps encouraged as many were by cynical British promises of emancipation—and this only added to the humiliation that their proprietor was to undergo.

Tarleton's attack had taken place on the cusp of May–June 1781, and Jefferson's term as governor expired in law on June 2. The election of a successor had been postponed for ten days because of wartime exigency, so Jefferson was only "acting" governor at the height of the crisis. Then, with perhaps too punctilious an attachment to legal form, he decided to rejoin his family. No doubt he hoped to avoid the suspicion of arrogating power to himself in an emergency, but he was instead suspected of something far more damaging. He had, in effect, technically left his post in a time of danger. This might have counted for less had not his governorship been a rather timid affair all around, with Jefferson always balancing between General Washington's demand for more troops and his own reluctance to enforce conscription on free citizens. People are seldom at their best when frightened and defeated, and the humiliation of 1781, blamed on himself, was to tar Jefferson with the coward's brush for the rest of his political career. This is notwithstanding a staunch, exhaustive, and successful defense of his own conduct, made on the floor of the Virginia House after the defeat and surrender of Cornwallis at Yorktown in October of that year. Had Jefferson only been governor during that last triumphant episode, everything might have been forgiven, but as it was he was generally associated only with the defeats and retreats of the war, and there is evidence that he never got over the bitterness of this. The contrast with Alexander Hamilton, who had served with distinction on Washington's staff and later led a gallant charge at Yorktown, was especially galling.

Cincinnatus, who quit high office in Rome and returned to his farm, was a known and revered model of conduct in those days, but the student of Jefferson nonetheless has the opportunity of becoming skeptical and even bored at the repeated disclaimers he made of any further interest in political life. He seemingly never tired of having to be persuaded and cajoled to take high office. However, in 1781 he does appear to have withdrawn with an overwhelming sense of hurt, and a settled determination to stay with his family, his books, and his ever-evolving Monticello, now even more in need of attention after the depredations of the at last defeated British Empire.

In his library, he took up the questionnaire that had been sent to him in 1780 by the French diplomat Francois Barbe-Menois. This document, which had also been forwarded to the governors of the other American states, inquired after a full profile of Virginia. It sought to know about its natural history, resources, population, and laws. There could hardly have been a better opportunity for Jefferson to show off, as well as to test, the extent of his knowledge. Though his *Notes on the State of Virginia* were not intended at first for publication, and were not read by other eyes until several years afterward (and then often in pirated and ill-translated form), this might be the point at which to review them.

Jefferson was not a man of the Enlightenment only in the ordinary sense that he believed in reason or perhaps in rationality. He was very specifically one of those who believed that human redemption lay in education, discovery, innovation, and experiment. There were many such in the American Revolution. Thomas Paine spent much of his career designing a new form of iron bridge to aid transportation and communication. Dr. Joseph Priestley, another man who fled royalist and Anglican persecution and who removed himself from England to Philadelphia after a "Church and King" mob had smashed his laboratory, was a chemist and physician of great renown. Benjamin Franklin would be remembered for his de-

ductions about the practical use of electricity if he had done nothing else. Jefferson, too, considered himself a scientist. He studied
botany, fossils, crop cycles, and animals. He made copious notes on
what he saw. He designed a new kind of plow, which would cut a
deeper furrow in soil exhausted by the false economy of tobacco
farming. He was fascinated by the invention of air balloons, which
he instantly saw might provide a new form of transport as well as a
new form of warfare. He enjoyed surveying and prospecting and,
when whaling became an important matter in the negotiation of a
commercial treaty, wrote a treatise on the subject himself. He sent
horticultural clippings from Virginia to the brilliant French consul
Crèvecoeur in New York, comparing notes on everything from po-
tatoes to cedars. As president, he did much to further Dr. Edward
Jenner's novel idea of cowpox vaccination as an insurance against the
nightmare of smallpox, helping Dr. Benjamin Waterhouse of
Boston—the initiator of the scheme in America—to overcome early
difficulties in transporting the vaccine by suggesting that it lost its
potency when exposed to warmth. Henceforward carried in water-
cooled vials, the marvelous new prophylactic was administered to all
at Monticello. (Not everything that Jefferson did on his estate was
exploitation.) For a comparison in context, we might note that Dr.
Timothy Dwight, then president of Yale and to this day celebrated
as an American divine, was sternly opposed to vaccination as a profane interference with God's beneficent design.

For all of his intellectual inquisitiveness, Jefferson lived in a time
when however much the interior human eye might strain itself it

could not see as far as the horizon so soon to be mapped by Darwin. It was still an age of pseudo-science, almost of alchemy as distinct from chemistry. Jefferson was able to see through some of the quackeries of the period—Mesmerism, for instance—but he was still a prisoner of the limitations of knowledge, as well as one who sought restlessly for a consistent explanation. Much of this no longer matters to us, but some of it was to do lasting and irreparable harm.

The great pseudo-scientist of the time was Georges Leclerc, the Comte de Buffon. This highly learned and industrious old fraud was considered the master of natural history and zoology, and had formed the view that North America was a wasteland condemned by nature. Its climate and soil were inhospitable to all but the scrawniest and most puny life: nothing was to be expected of it. We need waste no time on Buffon's theories except to say that they were rivaled in quasi-religious and creationist idiocy only by the opposing school. Baffled by phenomena such as the discovery of shells on high ground, "Neptunists" like Buffon proposed that the earth had emerged at different rates from a once-universal ocean, while their "Vulcanist" critics maintained that the shells had got there by propulsion from internal explosions. Since America had emerged late from the mother sea, Buffon argued, its plants and animals were as feeble and infantile as its Indian natives, and its immigrants would fall victim to the same etiolation and inanition. Buffon's emulators, such as the Abbé Raynal, inquired pityingly why it was that America had produced no poet, mathematician, or scientist worthy of the name. In patriotically seeking to refute this, Jefferson puts me in mind of Colonel Robert Shaw of the Massachusetts 54th Regiment. Shaw, one of the figurative heroes of Robert Lowell's poem "For the Union Dead," was killed at the head of his black troops during a hectic and gallant engagement in South Carolina, but not before he had written—in tones that Lowell might envy—that the former slaves under his command were fighting for "those whose poetry is not yet written." Jefferson phrased it like this:

> When we shall have existed as a people as long as the Greeks did before they produced a Homer, the Romans a Virgil, the French a Racine and Voltaire, the English a Shakespeare and Milton, shall this reproach be still true, we will inquire from what unfriendly causes it has proceeded, that the other countries and quarters of the earth shall not have inscribed any name in the roll of poets.

Jefferson's method, though, was one of taxonomic pedantry. He caught and weighed numerous animals, and he ordered the excavation of the skeleton of a mammoth, in order to prove to Buffon that if size mattered, then America was not lacking in the department of natural vigor. (To his credit, and in spite of lyrical passages in the *Notes* concerning the natural beauties of Virginia, he never argued that America was, in the sense of scale or profusion, superior.) But he never did solve the mystery of where the fossil shells had come from.

However, he did wish to insist that the American Indian was

fully the equal, in natural and innate ability, of any European. It is probable that, like many contemplative and unsoldierly types, Jefferson was very much impressed by the physical strength and martial ardor of these native peoples. He also admired their individuality and their deep knowledge of the wilderness: two "attributes" that were denied by definition to African slaves. At moments, also (and this trope is always latent in discussions of "race") he seemed to half-praise, and perhaps to half-envy, their sexual prowess. At any rate he maintained that if they could give up their strange idols and their primitive hunter-gatherer culture, they could readily assimilate. And at this point, a hideous problem began to obtrude itself, causing Jefferson to relapse into half-baked pseudo-anthropology.

How did the sons and daughters of Africa seem to take to servitude so readily? That, with its whiff of contempt, was in essence Jefferson's question. His study of antiquity had persuaded him that slavery was even more onerous at that period, yet Roman slaves like Epictetus, Terence, and Phaedrus had produced enduring works of art and science. "But they were of the race of white," he went on, as if "race" and color were the same, and as if Roman serfs had not been swarthy (and as if Buffon and Raynal had been onto something after all). His stupid first assumption led to a vicious conclusion, which he decided to safeguard with some qualifications as "a suspicion" that was only "hazarded with great diffidence." This was, however, that "the blacks, whether originally a distinct race, or made distinct by time and circumstances, are inferior to the whites in the endowments both of body and mind." In another aside, which gave off yet another whiff, he asserted that the sexual taste of black people for each other was comparable to the preference of the "Orang-Utan." Some commentators have attempted to excuse this expression, on the ground that "Orang-Utan" was a then common reference to a humanoid "wild man," supposedly "found" by explorers in trackless forests in Asia. But this would only be to restate the same unhealthy preoccupation in a different way.

It should be said in Jefferson's defense that he was not a "racist" or "racialist" in one sense, in that he did not for a moment believe that such putative or presumptive inferiority could be employed to justify slavery. Indeed, he was fond of pointing out to white fools that their own arguments would permit their own enslavement by any white person who could prove he was more intelligent or more educated than they were. So great was his conviction on this point that he broke a rule of Deism and spoke of divine retribution for the sin. "Indeed I tremble for my country when I reflect that God is just." But if one could presume a just God, what need would there be for human Enlightenment?

A bad conscience, evidenced by slovenly and contradictory argument, is apparent in almost every paragraph of his discourse on this subject. It is said that blacks must be deported at once after being freed, because of "ten thousand recollections of the injuries they have sustained." No more than a few lines later, Jefferson writes dismissively of slaves that "their griefs are transient." American white supremacists to this day maintain that blacks are "mud people" because their lack of conscience prevents them from blushing—they are not capable of summoning "blood in the face," as the Aryan Nations demagogues have it. Jefferson wrote: "Are not the fine mixtures of red and white, the expressions of every passion by greater or lesser suffusions of color in the one, preferable to that eternal monotony, which reigns in the countenances, that immovable veil of black, which covers the emotions of the other race?" Other more recent clichés of the duller sort seem to have found their first expression in the *Notes*: "In music they are more generally gifted than the whites with accurate ears for tone and time. Whether they will be equal to the composition of a more extensive run of melody, or of complicated harmony, is yet to be proved." (At this stage, Jefferson had not yet taught one of his children by Sally Hemings to be a maestro on the violin.)

More telling was Jefferson's honest insight into the sexual nature of the master-slave relationship. He phrased the dirty secret with remarkable candor: "The whole commerce between master and slave is a perpetual exercise of the most boisterous passions, the most unremitting despotism on the one part, and degrading submission on the other. The man must be a prodigy who can retain his manners and morals undepraved by such circumstances." To this he added that, even if blacks in their original state could not paint, or write poetry, they might improve on this want of natural talent if given a transfusion of white blood. But he never quite believed that black poets or black scientists, from Phillis Wheatley to Benjamin Banneker, were able to produce anything worthwhile on their own, or unaided by superior example.

When he embarked upon the *Notes*, Jefferson was still married to a white woman. Within a very short time, he was a widower. Martha died in September 1782, attended to the last by young Sally Hemings among others. Martha's death came partly in consequence of the birth of her sixth child, Lucy. It is recorded that, as she was expiring, she exacted a promise from Jefferson that he would never marry again. It appears that he was quite prostrated by her death, though it is also true that this calamity fell upon him just after the long series of defeats and humiliations that had attended the closing months of his governorship. Perhaps this combination explains the testimony of Monticello witnesses, who describe something very like nervous exhaustion. But perhaps not, in that he soon felt able to return to the fray.

The Congress, not long after his bereavement, renewed its invitation to him to become an envoy overseas. He was asked to join John Jay, John Adams, and Benjamin Franklin in Paris and help conclude a treaty with Britain. He accepted the offer but, having been delayed in his departure by ice-bound harbors on the eastern seaboard, found that his services would not be required after all. The Treaty of Paris had been concluded more swiftly than most had anticipated. Under the treaty, London recognized the independence of the United States, acknowledged American fishing rights up the coast of Canada, and conceded the territory that lay between the Alleghenies and the Mississippi. This large new tract of America meant that there was work to be done at home, and Jefferson was soon on his way to represent Virginia at the Confederation Congress. Arriving there and plunging into business, he was instrumental in having the Treaty ratified by a majority of the states (a fitting closure to the work begun by the Declaration). He also helped compose a congressional address on the stirring occasion of George Washington's retirement as commander in chief; a voluntary renunciation of power that straightened the shoulders and spines of every believer in republican virtue.

Expansion gave Jefferson an opportunity to indulge his two principal projects, which were the enlargement of the Union and the extension of democracy. Settlers were beginning to pour across the Alleghenies and to establish haphazard land claims. Communities such as the Kentuckians—at that time administered by Virginia—were beginning to see themselves as future states. Order was required, and Jefferson's mind was nothing if not orderly. He recommended that Kentucky become a self-governing state, and drew provisional maps, using a severe latitudinal grid, for fourteen more. This deliberately anticipated, indeed prefigured, further western expansion—though it is probably a mercy that Jefferson's projected state-names (which included Cherronesus, Assenenisipia, and Metropotamia) were rejected. The essence of the plan was gradual voluntary accession to the Union, rather than colonial government. Once again, Anglo-Saxon traditions were pressed into service, with Jefferson proposing that each new territory be divided into "hundreds," a hundred being ten square miles. He did not quite win this point, though the rectangular nature of American political geography still bears his stamp (and it was in this Congress, also, that he saw implemented his original scheme for a decimal dollar). Adult male suffrage was to be the rule for the new states, under what became known as the Ordinance of 1784, and considerable autonomy was allowed in return for recognizing the jurisdiction of Congress and the assumption of joint responsibility for the federal debt. On one point, however, Jefferson wanted uniformity of principle. He proposed that "after the year 1800 of the Christian era, there shall be neither slavery nor involuntary servitude." This was a bolder attack on the institution than any he had yet mounted, and on this occasion it was not the objection of southerners, potent as these were, that undid the plan. A New Jersey delegate was taken ill at a critical moment, and the motion was lost. Slightly contradicting himself where divine justice and retribution were concerned, Jefferson wrote: "Thus we see the fate of millions unborn hanging on the tongue of one man, and heaven was silent in that awful moment." Did he then tremble for his country at the thought that God was neutral?

Chapter Three

Revolution in France
(and a Meeting with Sally)

JOHN JAY HAVING completed his task in Europe, and having been appointed to be secretary of foreign affairs, Thomas Jefferson was the natural choice to succeed him as an American Minister Plenipotentiary overseas. He was to be headquartered in Paris, and to pursue the object of negotiating treaties and alliances with European nations. In the summer of 1784 he embarked for France, with his daughter Patsy and a small staff. There he joined John Adams and Benjamin Franklin in what must surely be the grandest team ever assembled by American or any other diplomacy. This distinguised constellation did not long endure—Franklin was infirm and had for some time wished to go home—and Congress at length decided to maintain only two ministers in Europe, Adams in London and Jefferson in Paris. From that moment on, Jefferson was to be engaged almost continuously in political life for a quarter of a century.

The Paris posting did not begin auspiciously. Jefferson succumbed to another bout of migraine, and learned of the death at Monticello of the infant Lucy, whose birth had hastened Martha's end. This awful news, however, at least came by the hand of a distinguished bearer—that of the Marquis de Lafayette, returning from a hero's tour in the United States. The Marquis was both well connected and well respected throughout Parisian society, and his friendship did something to alleviate misery as well as to enable access. Nonetheless, Jefferson was always careful, on being asked in distinguished circles if he was Franklin's replacement, to insist that nobody could replace the good Doctor—only succeed him.

America's position in Europe was in general a tenuous one. The British press, which was widely circulated, portrayed the new republic as a barbarous and chaotic experiment which showed every symptom of failure. American commerce was weak, and its military ability negligible (had not France had to fight many of the battles for its independence?). Credit was hard to come by, in consequence of the large debts incurred by Americans when they made borrowings to finance the revolution. Diplomatic representatives of the United States had to go obsequiously to Amsterdam bankers and plead for extensions on outstanding loans. Insults could be administered with impunity, as Jefferson discovered to his rage upon joining John Adams for a negotiation on a commercial treaty in London. Presented to King George III at a reception in March 1786, the two men were treated with abominable rudeness. It seemed that the volatile monarch (who had actually received Adams with courtesy on his initial appointment) had not forgiven or forgotten Jefferson's *lese-majesté* in the *Summary View*, let alone in the wording of the Declaration. Jefferson's careful revenge for this oafish regal conduct, exacted in the White House many years later, was to have considerable repercussions of its own.

America's attitude toward the French royal family was markedly different, since France had been such a staunch ally against Britain during the Revolutionary War, and since Benjamin Franklin had been practically lionized at court as well as in French intellectual and scientific circles. Nevertheless, Jefferson—who made several forays outside Paris, speaking to ordinary folk whenever he could—was very much aware that absolute monarchy was facing a crisis of reform if not indeed revolution. His friendship with Lafayette brought him into contact with those elements of the nobility—the Second Estate—who were willing to compromise with the Third Estate, or disenfranchised masses. (His attitude to the First Estate—the Catholic Church with its vast property holdings and its monopoly of religion, including official persecution of Protestants and Jews—can readily be imagined. In fact, we do not need to imagine it. When his daughter Patsy, enrolled in a convent school at the Abbaye Royale du Panthemont, wrote to him saying that she desired to become a Catholic and take her vows as a nun, Jefferson drove in a carriage directly to the school, removed her on the spot, and took her home.)

The corruption and decadence of the French system of society and economy did not outrage Jefferson merely as a spectator. Almost all trade and commerce was in the hands of the so-called "Farmers-

General," a state-supported cabal of propertied men to which was "farmed out" the right to levy taxes and imposts. One of Jefferson's tasks as minister was to open the French market to American imports, especially of tobacco—in which as a Virginia planter he took more than a patriotic interest. But the tobacco monopoly remained firmly in the clutches of the Farmers-General, and a series of exhausting negotiations on this and other commodities helped further to convince Jefferson that the monarchical system was fundamentally rotten.

For some time he seems to have believed that all that was required was a reform along American lines. In this he was encouraged by Lafayette, who kept a display copy of the Declaration of Independence in a double frame in his home, the second frame left empty "waiting for a declaration of the rights of France." And for a while, matters appeared to be proceeding along these lines, almost as they might have done, back across the broad Atlantic, if King George III had listened to reason. (In his reports to Jay in Washington, Jefferson depicted King Louis as fairly honorable but distinctly weak, and too much under the sway of his imperious queen, Marie Antoinette.) The monarch agreed to listen to deputations, to make reforming appointments, as of the liberal and rational Necker to the ministry of finance, and eventually to the first meeting of the three Estates since 1614. This assembly of the "Estates General" took place on May 5, 1789, with Jefferson in attendance in a visitor's gallery. In fact, he was something more than an interested bystander. As it became plainer that the assembly would not produce an amicable compromise between entrenched and insurgent interests, he proposed to Lafayette and others that a "charter of rights" be drawn up, and then promulgated by the king himself as a gesture of goodwill. Receiving a positive response, Jefferson drew up such a charter in person, enshrining habeas corpus, a free press, the opening up of the financial monopolies, and the right of the Estates General to make laws (albeit with royal consent). But the moment for any such bargain was past, and the king began to adopt a posture of intransigence. Again, Jefferson was inclined to lay the blame on the queen. As he later wrote:

This angel, as gaudily painted in the rhapsodies of Burke, with some smartness of fancy, but no sound sense, was proud, disdainful of restraint, indignant at all obstacles to her will, eager in the pursuit of pleasure, and firm enough to hold to her desires, or perish in their wreck. . . . I have ever believed that had there been no Queen, there would have been no revolution. . . . I should have shut up the Queen in a convent, putting harm out of her power and placed the King in his station, investing him with limited powers which, I verily believe, he would have honestly exercised, according to the principles of his understanding.

Reasonable though this may have seemed at the time and even in retrospect (and useful as a corrective to Burke's famously slavish paean to Marie Antoinette) it points up the very difficulty in which the constitutional and liberal aristocrats were to find themselves.

How likely was it, really, that King Louis would act in a more considered fashion with his wife imprisoned in a nunnery? Yet even after the breakdown of all negotiations, and the dramatic and stirring events of July 14, 1789, to which Jefferson was an eyewitness, he continued to identify himself with the Lafayette liberals, as it were. These liberals, despite occupying a position of extreme precariousness of which they remained largely unaware, were in fact quite revolutionary. The Marquis de Lafayette supervised the demolition of the captured Bastille, and gave its huge key to Thomas Paine to carry across the Atlantic as a personal gift to George Washington. He then proposed to the National Assembly a "Declaration of the Rights of Man and of the Citizen," one of the foundation documents of the modern world and a document that Jefferson had some share in drafting. This sense of being part of a grand and forward-looking enterprise helps explain the insouciance with which he greeted the lynching and dismembering of certain reactionary aristocrats, a price in blood he thought a small one to pay in the circumstances. After all, had not the Assembly at a stroke abolished all feudal and clerical privileges? Going some distance beyond his official duties as minister of a foreign power, in August he acted as host for a dinner organized by the Lafayette faction, where a discussion ensued that he recorded as "truly worthy of being placed in parallel with the finest dialogues of antiquity, as handed to us by Xenophon, by Plato and Cicero." The group decided that the king should stay in power, with an ultimate veto on legislation, but that the Assembly should be a single body. This was hardly the spirit of Philadelphia with its separation of powers. But, by the end of September 1789, Jefferson was safely on a ship and homeward bound. It would only be a short time before Lafayette and his noble colleagues would be in enforced exile, and Thomas Paine lying under sentence of death in one of Maximilien Robespierre's dungeons. Paradoxically, perhaps, Jefferson for a while grew fonder of the French Revolution as it became more extreme: this was to give a distinct inflection to the next stage in his political ascent.

Before we quit the scene of Paris, the subject of Sally Hemings must be considered. It was in Paris that Jefferson met her, and began an affair that was to continue for many years, produce many children, expose him to considerable scandal—and needlessly baffle generations of American historians.

Sally Hemings was the granddaughter of one white slaveholder and the daughter of another, John Wayles. Mr. Wayles was also the father of Thomas Jefferson's wife, Martha, so that the wife and the later mistress were in fact half sisters. To say that there was any taboo on "inter-racial" sex or "miscegenation" at Monticello would therefore be to exaggerate considerably. And, although she was certainly a slave by virtue of being Jefferson's legal property, Sally—as I shall now call her—had not been subjected to the indignities and humiliations of fieldwork and the lash. She was, from childhood, something more like a privileged housemaid. She had been in the room when Martha Jefferson died, and had heard Jefferson promise his dying wife never to marry again. Evidently she had blossomed in at least two ways since that time, and since Jefferson's departure for France. All reports speak of her as strikingly attractive (how nice it would be to have a portrait), and Jefferson's cousins, Francis and Elizabeth Eppes, thought highly enough of her general moral and mental deportment to entrust her with a mission of some responsibility.

This mission was to accompany his youngest surviving daughter Mary ("Polly") across the Atlantic in 1787. After the awful death of Lucy, Jefferson wanted the smallest one by his side. He gave orders that she was to be brought by a more senior female servant, who unknown to him had become pregnant in the meanwhile. So it was the fourteen-year-old Sally to whom the respectable and responsible Eppeses delegated the task.

The first clue to the relationship may lie in the simple fact that Jefferson, having met Sally and received his daughter from her in good condition, did not send her home again (as he had planned to do with the original escort). He did not require an extra servant at the Hotel de Langeac, his well-appointed residence, where Sally's brother James was already on the staff, being trained as a French chef. Possibly the latter consideration influenced him, in inviting Sally to stay on. But nor did he exactly need a governess, since both his daughters were destined for boarding school. Thus the beautiful Sally became a part of the ministerial household, with no specific duties. In 1788, Jefferson began to pay wages to her, and to her brother James, though he had never paid James a regular wage before. Moreover, slavery was not recognized as legal on French soil, a fact of which Jefferson was aware, and one that it would not have taken Sally long to find out. (In an act that was to alter Jefferson's life in myriad ways, the French Revolution was soon to abolish slavery in all French overseas territories as well.) It's therefore possible to say that, while they did have a common tie of affection and near-kinship in the person of the departed Martha—whom Sally may have resembled—Jefferson and Hemings did not have a "master-slave" relationship in the vile sense that is normally understood.

Most historians until recently took the view that a sexual liaison was literally unthinkable—certainly "unthinkable" in the sense that historians barely thought about it—for two reasons. The first was the revulsion that it is simply assumed that Jefferson must have felt, either for any carnal knowledge of a slave or (depending on the prejudices of the historian) any carnal knowledge of a black woman. In the case of Dumas Malone, whose enormous hagiography of Jefferson has been "standard" for far too long, one suspects that the historian had great difficulty considering the question of carnal knowledge at all. In status, Sally was barely a slave. And reckoning by "race," she was by descent and in appearance very nearly white. Jefferson was later to compose an insanely complicated ethnographical diagram to show how after a certain number of "crossings" between black and white the taint of Africa was removed. Sally was a "quadroon," and both she and three of her sons—the only slaves Jefferson ever freed—were able to register as "white" in the census of 1830. Most of their descendants continue to live on the "white" side of what is still America's most hazardous frontier, which surely qualifies Sally Hemings (whose grave now lies somewhere under the parking lot of the Hampton Inn at Charlottesville) as one of our Republic's Founding Mothers.

In her brilliant, dispositive study of the subject, *Thomas Jefferson and Sally Hemings: An American Controversy*, Professor Annette Gordon-Reed points out with well-controlled scorn that most analysts have refused even to consider whether Sally might have had a mind of her own, or might even more shockingly have made that mind up—in favor of an affair with a rich, famous, powerful, and fascinating man. We still fail to acknowledge or grant "agency," as modern jargon has it, to voiceless black female chattels. Unfortunately, Sally *is* still voiceless, and the sole volume of Jefferson's letters that might have contained correspondence with her is the only one in the whole vast set that has chosen to go missing. We do not even know if she was literate, though it seems probable, or whether she spoke any French, though this seems more likely. All we have is the testimony of her son Madison Hemings that she had while in Paris exacted a promise from Jefferson to free any children she had with him as soon as they achieved adulthood. And the "only" evidence for that promise is that he did indeed free them, all of them, and no other slaves, ever.

What of Jefferson's own, much better-documented character? That he was fond of beautiful women there can be no doubt, as his own wife and the wife of Mr. John Walker—offended husband in the first of the undenied Jefferson "scandals"—could well attest. So could Mr. Cosway, the English husband of the delightful Maria, with whom Jefferson carried on a passionate relationship during his time in Paris. We may not be sure about consummation in this case, but one of Jefferson's most emotional—or least unemotional—letters, on the rivalry between Heart and Head, was written explicitly for Maria Cosway. Not only was this the longest letter he ever wrote, but he composed it with his left hand, having broken his right wrist in vaulting over a fence to try to impress her. And there is another letter from him to her, dated April 24, 1788, in which we find the following:

> At Strasbourg I sat down to write to you, but for my soul I could think of nothing at Strasbourg but the promontory of noses, of Diego, of Slawkenburgius his historiaga, & the procession of the Strasburgers [sic] to meet the man with the nose. Had I written to you from thence it would have been a continuation of Sterne upon noses, & I knew that nature had not formed me for a Continuator of Sterne.

This is yet another Jeffersonian reference, very plain to him and evidently understood by Mrs. Cosway, to Laurence Sterne's *Tristram Shandy*, which contains a passage of distressingly unfunny linkage between noses and male sexual organs. Apparently, Mrs. Cosway did spot the reference and was displeased by it, and the relationship between them cooled, but this does not alter the fact that Jefferson was sexually knowing, fairly forward, distinctly eager, and without a mistress: the latter being an indulgence—at least in public—that his position as minister would have made awkward in any case. It was later in 1788, most probably, that Jefferson began his affair with Sally. From then on, she was paid wages, lodged in a separate boarding-house when he traveled out of Paris, and given some decent things to wear in a city that valued fashion. (Two hundred francs on "clothes for Sally" are noted in his accounts for April 1789.)

When they left for America, with Jefferson insisting that she be berthed next to him on shipboard, it has been suggested by some historians that Sally was pregnant, though the child, if there was a child, did not survive. But all her subsequent children, duly entered in the log of Jefferson's "farm book" at Monticello, were born exactly nine months after one of his much-punctuated sojourns at the house. No other possible father was present at all such times, which would seem to take care of the disgusting and unwarranted suggestion, made by several eminent historians, that Sally Hemings might have been giving or even selling herself to any male member of the Jefferson family. And all of the children were freed. It was hardly necessary, in light of all this, for the scientific journal *Nature*, in November 1996, to publish a detailed DNA analysis, conducted by three laboratories in isolation from one another and in ignorance of the identities involved, that showed an excellent match between blood drawn from Jefferson's and Hemings's descendants. Among other things, this precise genetic compatibility entirely excluded Peter and Samuel Carr, Jefferson's nephews, upon whom his white descendants, white society more generally, and "damage-control" historians like Douglas

Adair had been willing to place such circumstantial blame or suspicion as might accrue. Circumstances, remarked Emerson, are often persuasive as evidence—"as when you find a trout in the milk." But the evidence we now possess, which is to trout and milk what cream is to coffee, and something rather beyond that, leaves no space for any reasonable doubt.

The first person to make the "allegation" against Jefferson in his own lifetime was James Callender, a scandal-mongering journalistic hack who, having been useful to Jefferson in the past, had fallen out with him and become a propagandist for Federalism. Callender was an alcoholic thug with a foul mind, obsessed with race and sex. He referred in his articles to Sally as a "slut," to her children as a "litter," and to Jefferson as a man who would lecherously summon her from "the kitchen or perhaps the pigstye." Animal comparisons, suggestive of "miscegenation" as the equivalent of bestiality, are surely to be strongly deplored. Yet Dumas Malone, Jefferson's most revered biographer, continued in this tone as late as 1985, writing that for Madison Hemings to claim descent from his master was no better than "the pedigree printed on the numerous stud-horse bills that can be seen posted around during the Spring season. No matter how scrubby the stock or whether the horse has any known pedigree, owners invented an exalted stock for their property." Among many other offenses, this image quite crudely and directly inverts the real historic relationship between "owners" and "property." In other words, for many decades historians felt themselves able to discount Callender's story because it had originated with a contemptible bigot who had a political agenda. But one cannot survey the steady denial, by a phalanx of historians, of the self-evident facts without appreciating that racism, sexism, and political partisanship have also been manifested in equally gross ways, and by more apparently "objective" means, and at the very heart of our respectable academic culture.

Chapter Four

Interregnum

JEFFERSON'S ABSENCE IN France between 1785 and 1789 was very useful to his subsequent political rise. It won him high opinions as a diplomat and negotiator but, no less important, it kept him out of, and to some extent above, the domestic fray. Both the Constitutional Convention in Philadelphia and the rebellion mounted by Daniel Shays took place in his absence and allowed him the freedom to make comments without accepting responsibility. Most of his comments were in any case private, as befitted those of a senior envoy, though this did not prevent them from becoming widely known.

Shays' Rebellion, which was essentially a plebeian revolt against excessive taxation in Massachusetts, also confronted the new republic with the pressing issue of debt. And this in turn arose from the British policy of requiring American merchants to pay their bills in gold and silver. Like William Jennings Bryan more than a century later, Daniel Shays became the tribune of all the supposedly honest and toiling farmers who saw themselves oppressed by the enforcement of a credit policy dictated by an urban elite. From 1786 to 1787, men and boys from the agricultural areas of several states rallied to Shays, who had the credibility that attached to a former captain in George Washington's Continental Army. A strenuous effort on Washington's own part was required to repress the rebellion by means of the militia.

There were two possible points of view concerning Shays. One was that he represented the original antitax and antiauthoritarian spirit of 1776. The second was that he was a rabble-monger who threatened the whole basis of the new America. Jefferson in Paris was firmly of the first opinion. He wrote with great insouciance, to John Adams's wife, Abigail, "The spirit of resistance to government is so valuable on certain occasions, that I wish it to be always kept alive. It will often be exercised when wrong, but better so than not to be exercised at all. I like a little rebellion now and then. It is like a storm in the atmosphere."

When he wrote this, Jefferson had not heard the news of the bloodshed that accompanied the rebellion. But when he did hear such news, his insouciance was unpunctured. "What signify a few lives lost in a generation or two?" he wrote to Adams's son-in-law William Smith. "The tree of liberty must from time to time be refreshed with the blood of patriots and tyrants. It is its natural manure." The keyword here must be not "patriots," but "tyrants"— since the only candidate for the latter description was the government that Jefferson himself was serving as an ambassador. Later chroniclers have noticed an occasional tendency to a dismissive ruthlessness on Jefferson's part, when writing about the casualties inflicted by those of whom he approved. This tendency, which is probably necessary for leadership, can, however, always be expected to be quoted back at such a leader when he himself becomes the Establishment. (Conor Cruise O'Brien, the most mordant of Jefferson's critics, notes how unsqueamish he was about the repression of rebels he didn't like, such as the slaves in Haiti. O'Brien also observed grimly that Timothy McVeigh, when arrested after the Oklahoma City atrocity, was wearing a T-shirt blazoning the words: "The tree of liberty must be refreshed from time to time with the blood of patriots and tyrants." McVeigh's American fascist bomb was made largely out of fertilizer, which might also give pause to those who too easily compare blood with manure.)

McVeigh is not the only subsequent figure to have resurrected Jefferson's phrase and to have deployed it against the overmighty federal government. But the critical fact, in 1786–87, was that there *was* no federal government. Shays, in fact, had raised his standard only against the state government of Massachusetts, before being overcome by presidentially authorized militia troops. The need of the hour was a constitution that would allocate powers and responsibilities, as between the states and the center. The convention to determine and draft such a document was assembled in Philadelphia in 1787, in the absence of the star of the last Philadelphian show.

To say that Jefferson chafed at this enforced absence would be an understatement. He kept himself well informed, and in August 1787 wrote to John Adams expressing dismay at the secrecy to which the delegates had bound themselves (a secrecy he had found congenial enough when writing the Declaration):

> I am sorry they began their deliberations by so abominable a precedent as that of tying up the tongues of their members. Nothing can justify this example but the innocence of their intentions, and ignorance of the value of public discussion. I have no doubt that all their other measures will be good and wise. It is really an assembly of demigods.

This faint sarcasm served to conceal Jefferson's own division of mind about the value of the Constitution. Would it make the federal government too weak, or too strong? At first he thought, and wrote to Adams, that the "strong" element was too great, and had furthermore been overstated and overwritten. "How do you like our new constitution? I confess there are things in it which stagger all my dispositions." Recurring to Shays, whose shadow had indeed lain across the deliberations, he opined that "our Convention has been too much impressed by the insurrection of Massachusetts: and in the spur of the moment they are setting up a kite to keep the hen yard in order." Opposing the newfangled with the seasoned tones of a veteran, he added that "all the good of it" might as well have been "couched in three or four new articles to be added to the good, old and venerable fabric" of the Articles of Confederation (then only a

few years old), which he further described, oddly for such an icon-
oclast, as being as worthy of preservation as "a religious relique."

When writing to James Madison, one of the principal authors of
the essays that make up what we now call *The Federalist*, he took a
markedly different tone. The separation of the triune powers of executive, judiciary, and Congress impressed him favorably, and he was
not anxious for the future of the autonomous states, whose interests
he felt had been admirably balanced. But—and one must remember
that news of all developments reached him as an echo of the continuing debate—he was swift to borrow from the anti-Federalist
polemics in urging Madison to inscribe a Bill of Rights. His old Virginian ally thought this addition to, or amendment of, the Constitution to be superfluous. Jefferson argued that, on the contrary, a
written guarantee of certain rights (he did not choose to employ the
word *inalienable*) was a measurable advance. And he put forward another consideration, "one which has great weight with me: the legal
check which it puts into the hand of the judiciary. This is a body,
which if rendered independent & kept strictly to their own depart
ment merits great confidence for their learning and integrity."

In putting forward the case for a bill of rights and for judicial
review, as well as for autonomy and equality for the states, Jefferson
could not have known that he was making several rods for his own
future presidential back. But he did quickly discover that his various
suggestions, however confidentially intended, were being "leaked." In
his absence, America had become considerably more partisan and,
even though the Constitution itself made little if any provision for

political parties, this tendency was on the increase. In the short term, that made it harder for Jefferson to be on both sides of a question (as when he expressed the hope that ratification of the Constitution would be by a majority of states, while also giving voice to the contrary wish that some states, in the absence of a bill of rights, would decline to ratify at all). In the longer term, it prepared him for the more factional politics that had been inspired by the argument over Federalism.

These ambiguities in his own restless mind were very well expressed by a letter that he wrote to James Madison from Paris in September 1789. It may or may not be significant that he did not mail the letter, and did not hand it to Madison at their first meeting after his return from France, but eventually dispatched it to him in New York in January 1790. In it, he put forward the view that "the earth should belong only to the living generation," who ought to hold it "in usufruct," with as much right as an independent nation to be free of the trammels of preceding ages. He calculated the life span of a generation as nineteen years, and proposed that every kind of regime, law, and debt should expire at such intervals, thus renewing the human lease on the common treasury of the earth. Adam Smith had made a similar point, arguing that "every successive generation of men have an equal right to the earth, and to all that it possesses," but Jefferson's exchange with Madison is a curtain raiser for the grand confrontation, two years later, between Edmund Burke and Thomas Paine. Paine in his *Rights of Man* had proclaimed that "man has no property in man," an assertion that might have done very well as a statement against slavery, but which in fact denounced tradition and the hereditary principle as an enfranchisement of the dead over the living. Burke maintained that society was a contract between those departed, those alive, and those yet unborn, and Madison anticipated him by admonishing Jefferson. Was it not the case that previous generations had made roads and bridges, for the use of those who came afterward? Could it really be said that generations handed over to their "successors" regularly, every nineteen years? In *The Federalist*, in essays 47 to 51, Madison had already written a strict critique of Jefferson's draft constitution for the state of Virginia, of his concept of the separation of powers and of his view that disputes over the separation ought to be resolved by direct appeals to the people. This was no mere difference of emphasis: behind it lay sharply opposed concepts of government.

There seems to be no doubt that Jefferson had been profoundly influenced in this by the French revolutionaries, and by their zeal to make the world over again. This was to be pointedly symbolized by their abolition of the old calendar and their announcement of a new beginning for time. When he returned to the newly federalized United States, Jefferson brought with him a conviction that the revolution of 1789 was the continuation and confirmation of 1776, as well as the birth of a hardy ally for America against the continuing intrigues of Britain. If George Washington had understood all the implications of this, he might well not have extended to Jefferson, almost as soon as he had landed, the invitation to become secretary of state.

Chapter Five

Secretary of State

JEFFERSON YIELDED TO Washington's persuasion with his customary show of reluctance. He might have preferred reappointment to the post in Paris (as who would not have done, seeing the French Revolution apparently mounting in tempo and rhythm?). Alternatively, he might have liked to see to the upbringing and marriage of his daughters and the upkeep of his Monticello estate. He was about to be forty-six years old, a considerable age at that time. But he was hale and strong, a widower, and a man who had seen the world. He had been bitten hard by the political bug when overseas, and it was evident to him that the direction of American affairs could not be entrusted entirely to his rivals, even to his friendly ones.

This impression was reinforced when he took up his post, in the temporary capital of New York, in March 1790. The city had shown marked Tory tendencies even during the Revolutionary War, and now its salons seemed to reek of an American pseudo-monarchism, centered upon a too-courtly President Washington. Jefferson did not suspect Washington himself of kingly tendencies (or not at that stage, anyway), but he was certain that a sycophantic retinue was attempting to install a system of rank and title. Before leaving Paris, he had learned from Madison that John Adams proposed to style Washington as "His Highness, the President of the United States of America, and Protector of their Liberties," a mode of address that he (Jefferson) denounced as "superlatively ridiculous." The House, to his relief, preferred the plain form of "Mr. President," but the danger was not past. After all, Adams was now vice president, and might reasonably have hoped that any title of honor attaching to George Washington would later accrue, from either death or succession, to himself. It was a matter of shoring up Washington's democratic side and warding off temptation from other quarters.

Political factions did not then have predictable names, though the terms Federalist and anti-Federalist were in common circulation. When Jefferson sought to characterize partisanship, he did so by nationalizing the question and referring to the elitists and would-be aristocrats as "Anglomanes" or some other term expressive of nostalgia for the old country and its rule. In private, and sometimes in public, he quite accepted the corollary, which was the definition of a good American as a sympathizer with the revolution in France.

His time as secretary of state was an excellent dress rehearsal for his later years in office. The United States, still confined to the eastern seaboard, was faced with the maneuverings of three superior powers—Britain, France, and Spain—all operating on the same continent as well as dominating the high seas. To the west and inland, different Indian nations were ready to make alliances with whoever might seem to be on the winning side. Within the political boundaries of the new state, as the Shays' revolt had demonstrated, there was a strong connection between the greatest domestic problem—that of indebtedness—and the fluctuations of foreign policy. As a member of President Washington's inner circle, the others being Alexander Hamilton, James Madison, Henry Knox, Edmund Randolph, and John Adams, Jefferson's role was by no means confined to his own department of foreign relations.

One might describe the resulting conflict as a triangular one, though the triangle was by no means equilateral. Abroad, it was necessary to strike a balance between the three competing powers and to try to profit from any conflict between them. At home, it was necessary to avoid the predominance of any one faction that was too much aligned with any foreign power. And on the frontier, watch had to be kept for any opportunity to secure the Mississippi, without the possession of which, with its access to the vast interior, the "United States" could only hope to be a littoral power. Jefferson handled this three-sided dilemma in the following way. He encouraged any symptoms of jostling or jealousy between Britain, France, and Spain, while privately maintaining a strong prejudice in favor of the French. He identified the British interest, and its domestic conservative counterpart, with those like Hamilton who promoted a stern fiscal orthodoxy. And he surveyed the frontier for every sign of an opening, relying in the long run on his strong counter-Malthusian belief that Americans could outbreed all their rivals and—without exhausting supplies of food or other resources—fill up any vacuum with sturdy new settlers.

To say that this involved him in some rapid changes of principle and allegiance would be to put it very mildly. And one of the first battles had effectively been decided while he was still in transit from Paris. At the Treasury, Alexander Hamilton had proposed to consolidate the national or overseas debt with the debts owed by the states to the new federal government. This made economic sense in one way, but it put the smaller and less powerful debtors of the country at the mercy of speculators, who could purchase their bills at a discount. It also depended, as a matter of solvency, on stabilizing and maintaining the existing trade balance with Britain. Uncertain at which point to attack this alliance of interests, which could be defended at some level for its hardheaded soundness, Jefferson found himself at a disadvantage. "I arrived in the midst of it," as he later told the readers of his rather brief and cryptic *Autobiography*. "But a stranger to the ground, a stranger to the actors on it, so long absent as to have lost all familiarity with the subject, and as yet unsure of its object, I took no concern in it." This somewhat lame statement expresses the frustration he must have felt at the time, confined as he was to trying to persuade Congress to adopt a uniform scheme of weights and measures, and suffering as he had been from a renewal of his migraine attacks.

Alexander Hamilton soon came to realize that he faced a near-insuperable populist opposition to his plan for debt consolidation. It meant in effect a tax on poorer people in poorer (chiefly southern) states, for a greater federal good that lay some distance in the hypothetical future. Congress was deadlocked on the point. As it so happened, however, it was also deadlocked on another. The Constitution had mandated the creation of a national capital city, to be laid out on ten square miles of land. But it had not specified the location. One June evening in New York in 1790, Hamilton took Jefferson by the arm as they both approached the president's home on Broadway, and beseechingly walked him up and down. Nothing less was involved in the debt crisis, he insisted, than the survival of the Union itself. This was not an appeal that Jefferson could easily ignore, and he agreed to host a dinner on the following evening with himself as the referee between Hamilton and his chief congressional rival, James Madison. In a very early instance of American log-rolling and pork-barreling, it was determined at this dinner that Hamilton would get such votes in Congress as Jefferson and Madison could guarantee, and that to "sweeten the pill" for the southern states, the new capital of the country should be built on the Potomac, where Maryland and Virginia converged. This was to occur after a lapse of ten years for construction, during which time Pennsylvania could be soothed by having the nation's capital in Philadelphia.

Jefferson was later to deplore his own part in the making of this deal, which he claimed had riveted the "Hamiltonian system" of mercantile and banking supremacy onto the United States, at the expense of the honest agricultural interests that were always supposedly closer to his own heart. However, he could not have been unaware that Virginia had nearly voted not to ratify the Constitution in the first place—it eventually followed the commanding example of George Washington in so doing—and that his own region of that state (Albemarle County in the Piedmont district) remained resentfully anti-Federalist. Jefferson did not admire Patrick Henry, Virginian hero of the Revolution and leading opponent of ratification, half as much as he publicly said he did. He also understood that Henry's opposition to a strong central regime arose in part from his fear that it might lead to a government powerful enough to take measures against slavery: an issue that Jefferson was for the moment determined to postpone. Had he been present in Philadelphia and in the succeeding debates, it is difficult to imagine him taking a hard anti-Federalist position. But by helping to site the new capital so near to Richmond and Williamsburg, he could be sure of creating a Virginian interest in the huge new contracts that would follow and in the federal government that was distributing them. In addition, by offering his own aesthetic and architectural expertise to the builders and designers of the federal city, as he did with Pierre L'Enfant and others, he could hope to stamp his own personality on the seat of government and power. It was not a compromise that he was ever likely to have resisted. The selection of Washington as the site of the capital may have increased the specific weight of the slave states, but this alone cannot explain the way in which Jefferson encouraged Pierre L'Enfant's original street-and-boulevard plan, fired L'Enfant when his vanity went beyond control, engaged Thornton to design the Capitol, and eventually commissioned Latrobe to finish the task. Residents of the District of Columbia, such as myself, have some reason to be grateful to a sense of taste that, however calculated in its political origins, nonetheless transcended the bounds of its time.

Allying the feline skills of diplomacy to his natural talent as a committee man and infighter, Jefferson was one of the first Americans to try to ensure a good press for himself. This was a relatively simple matter at the time, since the public prints consisted mainly of three competing but malleable outlets. The first was John Fenno's *Gazette of the United States*, the second (rather confusingly) was Philip Freneau's *National Gazette,* and the third was the *General Advertiser,* edited by Benjamin Franklin Bache, the nephew of Old Ben himself. Fenno was a fairly determined advocate of Federalism. Bache was a man with an immense dislike and suspicion of George Washington, as was also shown in his paper the *American Aurora*, and Freneau was, as we might now say, up for grabs.

The art of leaking and influencing depends upon deniability, and Jefferson wanted to make sure that news from revolutionary France was favorably received and disseminated. This would help him, both in forwarding his anti-British foreign policy and in discrediting the "Anglomane" and hierarchical conservatives who were centered around Vice President Adams. In many ways, he was pushing at an open door. American opinion generally welcomed the French Revolution, both as a thing in itself (and a continuation of 1776) and as an assurance that at least one of the European superpowers would always be in the same corner as the small and vulnerable United States.

However, it was not really John Adams against whom Jefferson had to contend in this. It was George Washington. And Washington, whose instincts were as much conservative as they were liberal, and who enjoyed at least as much unquestioning public support as the French revolutionaries did, was not at all the man with whom Jefferson wanted to quarrel. Meanwhile, the actual tendency of events in Paris was one that removed influence from America's friends and allies, most notably the Marquis de Lafayette, and placed the fanatical and pitiless Jacobins in control. President Washington did not look upon this development with equanimity. Thus it came about that there was still another replay of the debate between Edmund Burke and Thomas Paine, this one conducted indirectly by warring American political factions, unofficially "led" by two senior members of George Washington's cabinet: Alexander Hamilton and Thomas Jefferson.

Hamilton easily won the first round. Fenno's *Gazette* chose to publish the first of Edmund Burke's attacks on the French Revolution, written in early 1790 and consisting of a near-hysterical speech to the British Parliament about anarchy and madness in Paris. It seems more than probable that Jefferson favored this publication, as something likely to discredit Burke as a fanatical Tory. For the rest of the time, he responded to any alarming news from Paris as the work of mere British propaganda, and by discreet use of the State Department's power to select which papers printed federal statutes was able to "manage" the public's reception of unfolding French events. However, Alexander Hamilton appreciated the value of British trade and of the British connection—still quite strong in the northern states—and took his own steps to ensure that government advertising, a prerogative of his Treasury Department, was allocated favorably toward the *Gazette*. This caused Fenno to alter his editorial tune in late 1790 (and reminds us again that our wigged and literate Founding Fathers were not immune to vulgar politics).

Chroniclers differ sharply on the extent to which George Washington was aware of, or interested in, these rivalries between his subordinates. (It is generally a mistake to assume that he was above the battle, or unconscious of it.) At any rate, and following the death of Benjamin Franklin in April of 1790, the president entrusted to Hamilton, rather than Jefferson, the handling of the many competing tributes that flowed to and from the National Assembly in Paris and the American Congress. The subtext of these flowery tributes and expressions of esteem was also a measure of the solidarity between France and America, and it seems plain that Washington did not desire to give any hostages to fortune until he could determine who exactly in France he might be dealing with. Jefferson may have bowed to the inevitable here, and may have partly liked the idea of an American conservative like Hamilton making the obsequies for France's favorite American, but he did not give up his part in the proxy war between Burkeans and Paine-ites.

This new "pamphlet war" became even more open a few months later. Thomas Paine's *Rights of Man*, an elaborate and contemptuous response to Edmund Burke's *Reflections*, was first published in London in February 1791. Its title page bore a dedication to George Washington. That was highly incautious, indeed presumptuous, in that Paine had not sought any permission to consecrate his book in this way. (He was later to develop a strong personal loathing for Washington, and to become convinced that the president had been indifferent to his imprisonment by Robespierre.) Jefferson compounded Paine's mistake, if only unwittingly. He received an early, borrowed copy of Paine's book, and wrote to an English friend: "We have some names of note here who have apostasised from the true faith: but they are few indeed, and the body of our citizens are pure and unsusceptible of taint in that republicanism. Mr. Paine's answer to Burke will be a refreshing shower to their minds." Going a little further, Jefferson forwarded his copy of Paine to a Philadelphia printer, with a covering letter, which said that he, the secretary of state, was "extremely pleased to find it will be re-printed here, and that something is at length to be publicly said against the political heresies which have sprung up among us. He has no doubt our citizens will rally a second time round the standard of Common Sense."

Apostasy, heresy . . . it is of interest to find Jefferson employing the language of faith when it comes to revolution. He was to repent it, so to say, because the edition of Paine's *Rights of Man* was thereafter printed, with his own signed note to the publisher attached as a preface. The first thing that then happened was that he received a visit from Attorney General Edmund Randolph, demanding to know if this endorsement had been with his permission, or not. Jefferson at once denied that this was the case, and subsequently (but only subsequently) wrote an extremely sycophantic letter to George Washington. He denied, possibly with justice, any advance knowledge of the use made of his letter. He also denied, with much less plausibility, any intention of offending John Adams, at any rate in public, by his use of the term "heresies." This was even though—as he self-righteously went on to tell the president—Adams, under the nom de plume of Davila, had been responsible for a whole series of essays hostile to the French Revolution. Washington did not choose to reply to Jefferson's lengthy apologia. Adams, however, did engage with him. He at first handsomely accepted Jefferson's written assurance, that publication of the note had not been deliberate. But he refused to swallow a later claim, that he himself had not even been the implied target of the "heresy" sentence. That was too much to ask him to credit (and was also directly contradicted by Jefferson's own letter to Washington). Adams declined further correspondence with Jefferson, on this point of honor, for many years.

Whatever view one takes of Burke's deepening pessimism and dogmatic adherence to the virtues of Church and King, whether in Britain or France, the fact is that after the summer of 1791 the Jacobins did their best to prove him right. William Short, a protégé of Jefferson's who had succeeded him in the Paris post, sent dispatches to the secretary of state, warning that old friends of America like Lafayette were being consumed by revolutionary fratricide. Jefferson, quite convinced that America's survival depended in large part on France, did not wish to hear bad tidings, and did his best to ensure that only good news from that quarter was printed in Freneau's *National Gazette*. By then he had become well aware that his rival Alexander Hamilton was also engaging in foreign negotiations as an aspect of domestic policy. A confrontation between Britain and Spain had occurred on the Canadian frontier, with the seizure by Spain of four British vessels in Nootka Sound. A dispute between London and Madrid, in Jefferson's view, would afford America the chance to extract concessions from both, and bring it within closer reach of the all-important Mississippi. But an actual war might be dangerous. The thing was to play off both against each other. This active neutrality was undercut by Hamilton's private meeting with the British envoy, Major George Beckwith—a man who viewed Paine's work with plain horror—at which Beckwith was assured that Britain would be favored, and Jefferson overruled, in the case of any outright conflict. The British, whose share of the American trade had actually increased since they lost direct imperial control, were distinctly grateful to know that there was, indeed, an "English party" within the American government. The British minister in Philadelphia, George Hammond, was able subsequently to assure his masters in London that Jefferson did not represent the united American view when he complained of British depredations on American commerce.

In May 1791, Thomas Jefferson and James Madison set out on an expedition that provided a rich vein of gossip at the time, and—which is the next best thing—has furnished matter for speculation by historians ever since. Under the pretext of a "botanizing tour," they left their customary haunts in Virginia and went to collect specimens up through the Hudson Valley and down through western New England. Keen though their interest in flora and fauna certainly was, they contrived to vary encounters with nature with private meetings at the homes of local anti-Hamiltonians. They had breakfast with Philip Freneau in New York City and took the opportunity to encourage him in his anti-Federalist journalism. They appear also to have interested themselves in Aaron Burr, whose populist campaign had unseated the "aristocratic" Dutchman Philip Schuyler—Hamilton's father-in-law—as the senator from New York. Jefferson and Madison did not manage, or possibly did not care, to meet Governor George Clinton, who was then emerging as an early model of the big-city political boss. But they were prospecting, if not indeed rehearsing, for an alliance between southern and northern anti-Federalists, against the hated party of England. Jefferson and Madison returned contentedly to Virginia, where Madison was to become the proxy voice of Jefferson whenever the latter felt the need to stay on the tactical sidelines.

A triumphant success for that "English party" was meanwhile to be seen in Hamilton's increasingly successful advocacy of a National Bank, regulating debt, trade, and securities and premised on the idea of a stable commerce with London and an abhorrence of revolutionary excess in France. Jefferson, when asked his opinion by Washington, insisted that the Constitution authorized no such thing. He feared the growth of an unaccountable center of power, a center with a somehow Anglomane character. Hamilton riposted—in the end, persuasively—that on this point the Constitution was open to imaginative interpretation rather than strict construction or "original intent," and that the clause awarding Congress all "necessary and proper" powers would meet the case. Jefferson, whose attitude toward deficit financing was strongly conditioned by his own disabling indebtedness as a Virginia planter, could never abandon the idea that there was something immoral, as well as unstable and sinister, in the idea of paper money and borrowing.

He began to employ a protégé of Madison's named William Branch Giles, a Virginia congressman with a slashing parliamentary manner, as a cat's-paw. Giles proposed a number of resolutions requiring Hamilton to produce vast amounts of Treasury data at the shortest possible notice. It was believed by the Virginians that Hamilton's rapid transfers of money and accounts must conceal something disgraceful, but in all cases the Treasury secretary outclassed his critics by furnishing true statements in conformity with near impossible deadlines. Frustrated, Jefferson drafted a general vote of no confidence in Hamilton, for his "maladministration," and used Giles to propose it in the House. With its defeat, his rural concept of fiscal integrity had been fairly easily eclipsed by Hamilton's mercantile modernism. Washington, and later the Congress, approved not only the setting up of the bank but the stewardship of Hamilton in general.

To this list of reversals for Jefferson could be added the appointment of Gouverneur Morris as American envoy to France. This crusty and peg-legged figure was regarded by Jefferson as "a high-flying monarchy man," and as yet another sign of George Washington's conservatism on the French question. But Jefferson decided to put all his faith in the moral and political inspiration of the Parisian revolution, which he hoped would spread over the world and thwart the well-laid plans of all conservatives, foreign and domestic. This conviction led him into some errors of overenthusiasm which he was to regret.

"The characteristic difference between your revolution and ours," as he was soberly informed by his old French friend the Comtesse de Houdetot, "is that having nothing to destroy, you have nothing to injure, and labouring for a people, few in number, uncorrupted, and extended over a large tract of country, you have avoided all the inconveniences of a situation, contrary in every respect." Much of the time, as is shown in his other writings, Jefferson would have applauded this view of the American Revolution as something *de novo*, as a new start in a New World, untainted by the barbaric residues of an *ancien régime*. France, however, was his reserve strength against the Hamiltonians and the Adamsians. It was also his intended counterweight to Britain. He pledged almost his entire credit on the Jacobin side of the scale. The pamphlet and newspaper combat between himself and Hamilton eclipsed in bitterness anything that had been printed during the years preceding the American Revolution. (It even led, in the long run, to the exposure of a wild and foolish dalliance between Hamilton and a scheming woman named Maria Reynolds. The author of that sordid but accurate report was one James T. Callender, whom we have met before.) Jefferson also made use of a phrase—later to become famous in a different context—when he spoke of "party animosities" as having "raised a wall of separation." Of Hamilton, the once penniless man who had immigrated from the West Indies and was rumored to be of "mixed" blood, he wrote with contempt to Washington that he was a person "whose history, from the moment history has stopped to notice him, is a tissue of machinations against the liberty of the country which has not only received and given him bread, but heaped honors on his head." Vast condescension of this kind gave rise in its turn to resentment against a "Virginia junta" with Jefferson as its chief.

However, in early 1793, it must have appeared to Jefferson that he had after all backed the right horse. The armies of revolutionary France easily repelled the invading alliance of panicky European monarchs, and in heady tones promised to export world revolution on republican bayonets. The reaction of American opinion was enthusiastically, even ecstatically, pro-French. The execution of King Louis in February was widely thought of as no more than natural justice, of the sort that had been applied to England's King Charles I. Most of all, the United States was not alone: it had a potent and magnificent ally. But there was a little chiaroscuro to be added to this brilliant picture. The more the cause of revolution advanced in Paris, the more America's old comrades in the city seemed to lose their eminence, or their liberty, or even their heads. Gouverneur Morris was cold and cynical on this point, in his generally counterrevolutionary reports to the State Department, and there were those among American conservatives who thought that, whatever might be the comparison with King Charles I, Jefferson was privately studying (as John Adams was to put it) for the role of a future American Cromwell.

William Short, now American chargé d'affaires in Paris, gave great distress to his patron by writing in pessimistic tones about the course of events there. And to Short, Jefferson wrote a riposte that re-creates the toxic fervor of the time:

> The Jacobins . . . tried the experiment of retaining their hereditary Executive. The experiment failed completely, and would have brought on the reestablishment of despotism had it been pursued. The Jacobins saw this, and that the expunging that officer was of absolute necessity, and the Nation was with them in opinion, for however they might have been formerly for the constitution framed by the first assembly, they were come over from their hope in it, and were now generally Jacobins. In the struggle which was necessary, many guilty persons fell without the form of trial, and with them some innocent. These I deplore as much as any body, and shall deplore some of them to the date of my death. But I deplore them as I should have done had they fallen in battle. It was necessary to use the arm of the people, a machine not quite so blind as balls and bombs, but blind to a certain degree. A few of their cordial friends met at their hands the fate of enemies. But time and truth will rescue and embalm their memories, while their posterity will be enjoying that very liberty for which they would never have hesitated to

offer up their lives. The liberty of the whole earth was depending on the issue of the contest, and was ever such a prize won with so little innocent blood? My own affections have been deeply wounded by some of the martyrs to this cause, but rather than it should have failed, I would have seen half the world desolated. Were there but an Adam and an Eve left in every country, and left free, it would be better than as it now is.

Reviewed through the prism of historical perspective, this disconcerting ruthlessness reads a little like the manifestos of later starry-eyed fellow travelers who felt that ultimate history had been attained by revolutions in Russia, China, or Cuba. Indeed, in the reference to Adam and Eve—yet another religious trope as applied to revolution—some extreme anti-Jeffersonians have even detected a prefiguration of Cambodia's "Year Zero." More important was the way in which Jefferson automatically translated the import of French events into their significance for American ones. As he went on to claim to Short, no less a person than George Washington took an identical view:

He desired me therefore to write to you on this subject. He added that he considered *France as the sheet anchor of this country and its friendship as a first object.* [Emphasis in original.] There are in the US some characters of opposite principles; some of them are high in office, others possessing great wealth, and all of them hostile to France and fondly looking to England as the staff of their hope. These I named to you on a former occasion. Their prospects have certainly not brightened. Excepting them, this country is entirely republican, friends to the constitution, anxious to preserve it and to have it administered according to its own republican principles. The little party above mentioned have espoused it only as a stepping stone to monarchy, and have endeavored to approximate it to that in its administration, in order to render its final transition more easy. The successes of republicanism in France have given the coup de grace to their prospects, and I hope to their projects.

This admonition to Short greatly overstated George Washington's partisanship for France, but it did not overstate—or not by much—the general American feeling that the Jacobins were making European history, and even European geography, in a fashion closer to the heart's desire. This exciting prospect perhaps allowed Jefferson his subjective and objective coldness about the fate of those disposable "friends" of his (such as Thomas Paine, who had got into great trouble in France for publicly opposing the death sentence for King Louis, an event written down by Jefferson above as "the extirpation [of] that officer"). After all, were not John Adams and Alexander Hamilton quaking at the number of feasts, bonfires, and celebrations erupting across the United States in solidarity with the cockades of Liberty, Fraternity, and Equality?

This moment of Jeffersonian exhilaration was not to last long. For one thing, no sooner had the French revolutionaries decapitated the king of France than they declared war on the king of England. To the disturbing question of the proper American response to an outbreak of war was added the embarrassment of a new French envoy, hotfoot from the new regime in Paris and naively convinced that America was a place where his welcome could never be worn out. This was Edmond Charles Genet, a man whose advent on the scene was a brilliant fusion of tragedy with farce, both these elements being at Jefferson's eventual expense.

Here is how matters stood, or had stood until 1793. The United States had a treaty of alliance with France, dating back to 1778 as the seal of Franco-American brotherhood in the Revolutionary War. It had also had a commercial accord with France, dating from 1786, which in case of war mandated that French belligerent vessels would receive favored treatment in American ports. However, the United States was also in constant negotiation with Britain to regularize commercial and military relations, and to try to negotiate an end to the British practice of impressing, or kidnapping, sailors off American ships. Hamilton and the other friends of England argued that the treaties with France no longer applied, since they had been made with the previous monarchical regime. Washington split this difference by issuing a "Proclamation" declaring the United States "impartial" (but not, as Hamilton had wished, "neutral"). Jefferson wanted two things at the same time: for America to profit from any Anglo-French war, at least by supplying both sides with "neces-

vateer had left anchor before any decisive action could be taken. Revenge was exacted instead on the French minister, whose appointment Jefferson now suddenly viewed as "calamitous." He agreed to write a lengthy letter to Paris demanding Genet's recall. The response to this diplomatic *démarche* was further proof of the way that matters were progressing in Paris. Genet, for all his revolutionary posturing, had been a member of the Girondin faction and was out of favor with the regnant Jacobins. Those in power would have been quite happy not just to recall him but to place his neck under the guillotine. Genet finally elected to stay in America, where he married the daughter of Governor George Clinton of New York and, remaining in this respect at least a Jeffersonian, took to the pacific pursuit of agriculture.

The general discredit which all this inflicted on the prestige of the French Revolution was a specific discredit to Jefferson personally. He had all he could do to limit the damage. In the face of a tremendous public outcry at Genet's depredations, the cabinet voted to publish the papers connected with the affair. Jefferson, whose job it was as secretary of state to see to this, managed to insert some equally damaging material about British naval threats to American trade. Thus, very narrowly indeed, he escaped the general wreck of the French faction, and was even able to appear as one who could subordinate his personal sympathies to the requirements of his country. As a coda to his time as secretary, he submitted to Congress a lengthy and brilliant "Report on American Commerce." In this document, he put forward the idea of an America committed to international free trade, tied to no nation, and ready to employ economic rather than military means of coercion. Borrowed in some degree from Adam Smith's *Wealth of Nations*, the report was also intended as an alternative to Alexander Hamilton's pro-British mercantilism.

He then announced that he was returning to Monticello and abandoning the political arena for good. The thing seemed superficially plausible: Jefferson had by now reached the half-century mark in his life, and his russet hair was turning gray. To his friend and co-conspirator James Madison, who implored him to reconsider, he described the condition he was fleeing:

> Worn down with labors from morning to night, and day to day; knowing them as fruitless to others as they are vexatious to myself, committed singly and in desperate and eternal contest against a host who are systematically undermining the public liberty and prosperity, even the rare hours of relaxation sacrificed to the society of persons in the same intentions, of whose hatred I am conscious even in those moments of conviviality when the heart wishes most to open itself to the effusions of friendship and confidence, cut off from my family and friends, my affairs abandoned to chaos and derangement, in short giving everything I love, in exchange for everything I hate.

This adamantine posture, far exceeding what came to be known in American politics as a "Sherman declaration," may have convinced

George Washington, who had urged him not to resign sooner and had indeed postponed his own resignation as part of the bargain that kept him on, but it did not at all impress men like John Adams, who were already heartily sick of Jefferson and his striking of sensitive and superior attitudes. It is possible that Jefferson might have really meant it this time, because his period as secretary of state had been deeply wounding and frustrating, and because his last months in office were further overshadowed by a ghastly outbreak of yellow fever in Philadelphia, which poisoned local existence and almost paralyzed the government. The cool mountains of Albemarle County must have beckoned as never before. Nonetheless, he must also have been acutely aware that he left America stalemated, as between Federalists and Republicans, as between England and France, and as between the putative heirs of the aging George Washington.

Above all, perhaps, the French Revolution had lost its charm for him. And this was for a paradoxical reason. His hope for a rapid spread of French revolutionary ideals had been realized—but not in a way that he welcomed. Almost as soon as the Rights of Man had been proclaimed, with his own assistance, in Paris in 1789, they migrated across the ocean to the island of Hispaniola and that part of it which, then named Saint-Domingue, is now called Haiti. This French colony was run by a white planter class and produced an immensely profitable sugar crop with the work of a mass of imported African slaves. A smaller class of *gens de couleur*, or those of mixed parentage, played an intermediate role. It was, initially, their rebellion against white power that precipitated a larger-scale slave revolt in 1791. Although Jefferson at first took no strong view of this development, and routinely referred to the racial elite in Haiti (as I shall call it) as "aristocrats" and "monocrats," he did take alarm when he saw that there might be a full-dress black slave revolution so near to the American South. As secretary of state, he saw this not as the second revolution of liberty in the hemisphere, but as a frightening development that had sent white French planters to seek refuge in places like Charleston, South Carolina. The force of the comparison was not at all lost on him, as he wrote to James Monroe in July 1793:

> The situation of the St. Domingo fugitives (aristocrats as they are) calls aloud for pity and charity. *Never was so deep a tragedy presented to the feelings of man.* I deny the power of the general government to apply money for such a purpose, but I deny it with a bleeding heart. It belongs to the State governments. Pray urge ours to be liberal. . . . It will have a great effect in doing away the impression of other disobligations towards France. I become daily more convinced that all the West India islands will remain in the hands of the people of colour, & a total expulsion of the whites sooner or later take place. It is high time we should foresee the bloody scenes which our children certainly, and possibly ourselves (south of Potomac) will have to wade through, & try to avert them. [Italics added.]

Thus, not only do we find Jefferson's heart bleeding for a slave-holding caste, but for their plight as a tragedy so deep as to have no parallel. He is urging his fellow Virginian to find public money to succor and sustain these refugees from the ideas of 1789. (Perhaps not exactly of 1789; the French regime did not formally abolish slavery until 1794, the following year, but by then slavery had been destroyed in Haiti at any event.) Jefferson also hopes that such charity will conciliate French opinion after the bruising it has undergone at American hands, and one may note that this letter to Monroe is sent in the very month that "Citizen" Genet has at last been disowned—by Jefferson himself.

It is of some interest also to know that Genet had been a member of the Parisian political club known as *Les Amis des Noirs,* along with many of his fellow Girondins, and that Jefferson in the period before 1789 had been approached to endorse this club but had declined. Genet's anti-slavery sympathies, indeed, had been used to discredit him among southerners during the time that he was envoy to America. So Jefferson took the same view of Haiti as he had of Virginia: the abolition of slavery could be as dangerous and evil as slavery itself. He did not, through this blinker of prejudice, at first discern that events in Haiti would one day provide him with an opportunity of historic dimensions.

Chapter Six

In Waiting

IN RETREAT AT Monticello from the earliest days of 1794, Jefferson may possibly have intended to keep to his retirement. In the fall of that year, he certainly declined an invitation from Edmund Randolph, who had succeeded him as secretary of state. Randolph wanted him to be the negotiator with Spain for a new treaty. Jefferson did not merely refuse the offer but added that no inducement of any kind could tempt him back into politics. Yet it might equally well be argued that he was reserving himself for something more advantageous.

It was during these years that, under the spur of economic exigency, he retrenched and modernized his famous home. He remained an agrarian, in his newly designed plow, modeled on an earth-cutting technique that he had first noticed when in France, and in his importation of a more efficient threshing machine from Scotland. He made some concessions to industrialism by establishing a nail-making factory on the estate and organizing the younger male slaves into a rudimentary production line. A spacious reconstruction of the Palladian house was put in hand, still somewhat revealing to the visitor's eye in that some of its innovations (the dumbwaiter, the revolving door, the views from the windows) were so arranged as to minimize any direct contact with the slaves themselves.

Having passed the age of fifty while secretary of state, Jefferson was being made a grandfather by the birth of Martha's children to Thomas Mann Randolph. And he himself became a father once more, with the arrival of Sally Hemings's first recorded child in 1795. Mentally and physically he remained exceedingly young and hale for his years, and took regular strenuous exercise on horseback and with his trusty gun. How likely is it that he could for long have avoided the political imperative? Only, perhaps, if members of his own political faction had held the upper hand in the nation's business. But by the closing months of 1794, the news (and his own correspondents) told him that such was not the case. A revolt, known to history as the Whiskey Rebellion because of its protest against a federal excise on liquor-distilling, broke out in western Pennsylvania. The political leadership of this movement, which took its tune from the French Revolution, at one point proposed to call itself a "Committee of Public Safety" along Jacobin lines. George Washington, Alexander Hamilton, John Adams, and John Jay, for their part, had no difficulty in detecting the subversive hand of the recently formed, Republican-leaning "Democratic Societies." These they darkly termed "self-created societies"—as if there could have been any other kind. The militia was summoned from several adjoining states, and a force of fifteen thousand men, with Hamilton as one of its commanders, was put into the field against the radicals. This exercise in overwhelming authority had the effect of crushing the rebellion with impressive speed.

It also had the effect of outraging Jefferson. In a letter to James Madison, leader of the Republicans in Congress, he characterized the president's rhetoric as "an attack on the freedom of discussion, the freedom of writing, printing and publishing." He resorted again, as he had with the precedent of the Shays' Rebellion, to the image of a permanent contest between liberty and tyranny. The administration was "monarchical," its worldview "perfectly dazzled by the glittering of crowns and coronets." Exaggerating the situation somewhat, he also thought he saw a tendency to separatism among the rebels, which if too roughly handled would imperil the Union.

On the very same day, November 19, 1794, that Washington made his attack on the "self-created" societies, his Chief Justice John Jay signed a treaty in London. When the terms of the agreement with Britain became known, a huge patriotic and populist reaction was ignited. The British agreed to evacuate their positions in the American Northwest, which was little more than they had undertaken to do in 1783. Americans were to be allowed to trade unhindered with the British East Indies but not with the closer West Indies. Competing claims for losses in earlier conflicts were settled, but very much to the advantage of British creditors. Above all—and easily grasped by public opinion—the British declined to make any undertaking about their much-resented impressments, or virtual kidnappings, of American seamen.

Here, to Jefferson, was the overseas counterpart of Washington's and Adams's domestic Anglomania: "a treaty of alliance between England and the Anglomen of this country against the people of the United States." It seemed almost like treason, the consummation of the despised Hamiltonian "system." No effort had been made to use America's commercial leverage, as Jefferson had advocated in his closing months as secretary of state. Moreover, no advantage had been taken of Britain's highly unfavorable military position as against the French, who had lately been carrying all before them on the European mainland. There is a hint, in a letter that Jefferson wrote in April of 1795, that this latter consideration might after all draw him out of Monticello. To William Branch Giles, a senior Republican congressman and his old colleague in the anti-Hamilton contest, he wrote:

> I sincerely congratulate you on the great prosperities of our two first allies, the French and Dutch. I should have little doubt of dining [in London] with Pichegru [the triumphant French general] for I believe I should be tempted to leave my clover for awhile, to go and hail the dawn of liberty and republicanism in that island.

If Jefferson would go to London, even in jest, to celebrate the reawakening of 1776 and 1789, might he not venture as far as

Philadelphia? His tone was somewhat less jaunty several months later, when the Republicans in Congress performed unexpectedly badly in their attempt to block the Jay Treaty. Then, on September 19, 1796, came the publication of what everyone knew was coming but nobody had really prepared for—the "Farewell Address" of President George Washington. To all Republicans it became instantly apparent that there was a vacuum, both in national power and in their own leadership.

It was very clear to Jefferson that Vice President John Adams would be the probable winner in any election to succeed Washington, and he may in any case have preferred (as he said he did) this outcome. There was something to be said for avoiding any immediate comparison with the Father of the Country; something to be said also for avoiding the charge of vaulting ambition. However, the party would not be gainsaid, and, having informed Jefferson that he would not in any case be a candidate himself, James Madison arranged with the Republican leadership that a caucus would simply declare Thomas Jefferson and Aaron Burr as the candidates. The election proceeded in a stately fashion on what might be called this assumption. It is perhaps both heartening and sobering to reflect that, in the contest between Jefferson and Adams in 1796, the electors were offered a choice between the president of the American Philosophical Society and the founder of the American Academy of Arts and Sciences, and chose both of them.

At that date, the Electoral College was determined by each state's presidential electors, themselves chosen by state legislatures, each of whom could cast two votes. One such vote had to be for a candidate from another state. The two candidates receiving the most votes became, regardless of party, president and vice president respectively. The campaign of 1796 was short but by no means sweet. Despite Jefferson's almost Olympian detachment from the process, he was subjected to a series of vitriolic assaults by poster and pamphlet, accusing him of being an atheist, an abolitionist, and a sympathizer with bloody-handed Jacobinism. The element of truth in all three accusations is retrospectively amusing, given their authors' failure to appreciate Jefferson's patient genius for compromise. He did not even mention the election in his letters, and when the votes were counted was gratified to see that John Adams had received 71, with himself a creditable second with 68. Adams's co-Federalist Thomas Pinckney had received 59 votes, while Aaron Burr had to content himself (or rather, further discontent himself) with an embarrassing 30.

With Washington departed, American politics swiftly became more openly factional. At first, both Adams and Jefferson strove to keep this partisanship within bounds. Jefferson decided not to send Adams a letter of congratulation in which he had criticized Alexander Hamilton. Adams generously proposed that Jefferson lead a high-level mission to France, to soothe Parisian fury at the John Jay treaty with England. (The new vice president declined the honor, preferring to chair the Senate and eventually writing a short, elegant book on order and procedure that is still in use.) The inauguration of both men was conducted amicably. But none of this could dilute the distrust that the two men felt for each other, and had felt ever since the Burke-Paine controversy of 1791, and none of it could obliterate the plain fact that they saw Anglo-French rivalry, and its domestic equivalents, from perspectives that were entirely opposed.

Adams's interpretation of "neutrality" took the form of a call for military preparedness—but directed principally against France. In 1797 he delivered a speech denouncing French threats to American interests. He then sent a team of three negotiators to Paris, two of them Federalists (Charles Pinckney and John Marshall) and one (Elbridge Gerry) a Republican. In their dealings with the great cynic and survivor Talleyrand, now foreign minister, these three were made aware that they had three French counterparts who were soliciting a large bribe as the price of diplomacy. The French trio—Jean Conrad Hottinguer, Pierre Bellamy, and Lucien Handeval, ominously described as agents X, Y, and Z in the American report home—also wanted President Adams to repudiate his anti-French remarks. This combination of cupidity and arrogance was, when revealed by Adams to an infuriated public, an occasion for public outrage that quite canceled the earlier reaction to the Jay sellout. (Since it was the Republicans who had first incautiously demanded that Adams release the incriminating papers, the effect was doubled if not quadrupled.) "Millions for defense, but not one cent for tribute," became the cry. Taking full advantage of the moment, Adams proposed to expand America's armed forces and to create a Navy department. This was especially galling to Jefferson, who was forced to oppose in public something that (for other reasons, as we shall see) he had long privately endorsed.

But his position in that argument had been fatally undermined from another quarter. While still in private life, in April of 1796, he had given an immense hostage to fortune by writing what he supposed was a private letter to Philip Mazzei. This seemingly harmless Italian viticulturalist had been invited to Monticello to assist Jefferson in his lifelong scheme to get Virginian wine up to standard. The letter contained a digression into American politics, in which Jefferson made his usual contemptuous allusions to that "Anglican, monarchical, & aristocratic party . . . whose avowed object is to draw over us the substance, as they have already done the form, of the British government." Jefferson felt that this "party" comprised "the Executive, the Judiciary" and "all the officers of the government, all who want to be officers, all timid men who prefer the calm of despotism to the boisterous sea of liberty." If this was not comprehensive enough as a depiction of the Washington administration, he went on to tell Mazzei, "It would give you a fever were I to name to you the apostates who have gone over to these heresies, men who were Samsons in the field and Solomons in the council, but who had had their heads shorn by the harlot England." (Once again, one is compelled to notice his use of religious and biblical imagery when discussing articles of revolutionary faith.)

It was to prove a disaster for Jefferson that Mazzei translated the letter into Italian and published it in an Italian newspaper. The text was seized upon by a French newspaper and translated into French, picked up by an English journal which put it into English, and in this Babel-like form transmitted across the Atlantic and waved in the face of its original author. His opponents made the largest possible use of the unmistakable slur on the character of Washington, who still occupied the pedestal of immunity and had acquired the additional honor of a man who had unostentatiously retired. Seeing his own honor widely impugned in turn, Jefferson was impaled on both horns of a dilemma. In the first place, he *had* written the letter. So, in order to demonstrate that it had been somewhat mangled in translation (he had for example said the "forms of the British government," not the actual "form" of monarchy itself) he would have been obliged to open much more of his correspondence to the public view. And his natural self-pity when it came to abuse in the public prints, the self-pity that often made him seem to himself to be too dignified and principled for the rugged business of politics—why, this would not long survive the revelation that he had his own paid hacks in the American gutter press. He therefore preserved a stony silence that did him no good at all. And it seems certain that, after this controversy, he never spoke or corresponded with George Washington again.

Jefferson's view was that those who shouted the loudest about "foreign influence" were themselves the principal agents of it. He never ceased to suspect that Hamilton was planning something like a pro-British coup. In the chair of the Senate, he was often exposed to the most extreme abuse, both of himself and of rival factions by one another. He made a significant comment on one such quarrel, which had seen a Connecticut Federalist and a Vermont Republican move from insults to blows. "These proceedings," he observed drily, "must degrade the General Government, and lead the people to lean more on their state governments, which have been sunk under the early popularity of the former."

This prescient and ever-present thought, about the relative integrity of the states, was to prove his secret weapon in the next great political combat. Stirred by seaborne confrontations between French and American ships, and roused to a high pitch of moral indignation by the "XYZ" affair (and the apologetic posture adopted toward it by Jefferson and other Republicans), the supporters of Adams and Hamilton overreached themselves. They whipped up what would have otherwise been called, had it not had any French taint, *une grande peur*. Spy fever, hatred of foreigners, invasion scares—nothing was spared. The new national song "Hail Columbia" deposed "the Marseillaise" as a popular favorite. The state of "quasi-war" with France was to be reinforced by a standing army, taxes to support it, and an internal siege of constant vigilance. It was even proposed that there be an Anglo-American military alliance to take over Spanish America. In this febrile atmosphere, Congress rushed to pass the Alien, Sedition, and Naturalization Acts.

Taken together, this parcel of emergency laws gave the president the power to imprison or deport any "alien" of an enemy country in time of war, or indeed any noncitizen of any country if such a person was held to endanger national security. It lengthened to fourteen years the time that an immigrant had to spend before becoming a citizen. And it permitted the punishment of anyone who, by publishing or utterance, brought the government of the United States into disrepute. (Or most of that government: the Sedition Act actually exempted the person of the vice president from the list of those officials who were above such criticism.)

Not stooping to notice the blatancy of that last provision, Vice President Thomas Jefferson at first took his stand on two points. First, he thought the measures struck directly at foreign radicals and dissidents who had until then thought of the United States as their second home. He had in mind such men as the French philosophe Constantin Volney, whose anticlerical masterpiece *The Ruins* he had helped translate, or the Polish hero Thaddeus Kosciusko, volunteer general in the American Revolutionary War. Both men felt compelled to leave the country they had honored by their presence. Second, he regarded the laws on publication and advocacy as a flat-out negation of the First Amendment to the United States Constitution, and thus as beyond the jurisdiction of Congress. As a slight concession, the Federalists amended the proposed law to exclude "prior restraint" of publication, but they did pass it in a triumphalist manner on Bastille Day 1798, and they did enforce it with some rigor against Republican editors and pamphleteers.

Against this arrogation of arbitrary power at the center, Jefferson knew that he could in the last resort—as he had hinted in the Senate— deploy the weapon of "states' rights." The record should reflect that, when he did choose to do this, he did not do so lightly. To his Virginia friend John Taylor he at first wrote in phlegmatic tones, viewing party warfare as inevitable and deploring the idea that the losing side should threaten the Union. "A little patience," he wrote, "and we shall see the reign of witches pass over, their spells dissolved, and the people recovering their true sight." The exasperated Taylor decided to take Jefferson up on one of his ethereal and theological images. If witchcraft was in fact the problem (and "witch-hunt" has been the preferred metaphor of American panic from Salem until now), then it followed that "the spell must be broken by incantations on the part of the Republicans." He pungently reminded Jefferson that, under the original Philadelphia compact, powers not awarded to the federal government were held to reside in the states, or the people. If now was not the moment for such a Republican rejoinder, then when?

Taylor might not have selected Alexander Hamilton as his preferred example, but Hamilton had indeed written, in *The Federalist*:

> It may safely be received as an axiom in our political system that the State governments will, in all possible contingencies, afford complete security against invasions of the public liberty by the national authority. . . . They can discover the danger at a distance; and possessing all the organs of civil power, and the confidence of the people, they can at once adopt a regular plan of opposition, in which they can combine all the resources of the community. They can readily communicate with each other in the different States, and unite their common forces for the protection of their common liberties.

Not for the first time, Jefferson may have felt a slight sense of freedom resulting from his absence in Paris during the argument over the Constitution. He occupied a certain point of balance as between traditional, dogmatic anti-Federalism and the more improvised kind. In concert with James Madison, he helped draft resolutions from two states, negating the Alien and Sedition Acts. I say "negating" because there is a narrow but deep difference between the two resolutions. The Kentucky version, drafted by Jefferson himself, in effect "nullified" federal law as it applied within that state's borders. The Virginia resolution, more influenced by Madison, is used by scholars of constitutional law to define the doctrine of "interposition." On this reading, a state may shield its own citizens from federal rulings and invite other states to decide on the legality and justice of the matter. (This nicety and nuance did not prevent Alexander Hamilton, who had come ever more to the fore as a military figure in the Adams administration, from proposing the dispatch of federal troops to Virginia to show who was in charge.)

Thus, within the space of two years, Jefferson had been arraigned by pro-slavery forces as an abolitionist and had furnished the moral rhetoric of states' rights that was to become the great political prop of the pro-slavery faction. In the course of the same row, he was to hand his enemies a lash that he would feel in his own lifetime. One of the Republican journalists caught in the mesh of the Sedition Act was that genius of scurrility, James Callender. This exile son of Scotland wrote so viciously against targets like President Adams and Alexander Hamilton that he was prosecuted and later imprisoned.

Jefferson, seeing the man's talent and feeling for his plight, offered him discreet financial subventions and took him into confidence as a man who might one day prove useful. He thereby launched the career that would culminate in the first lurid exposé of his own affair with Sally Hemings.

The potential conflict between states' rights and High Federalism never reached a point of open crisis and confrontation. By means of those coincidences that give accident its necessary place in the telling of history, two simultaneous events supervened. The first of these was the full assumption of power, in France, by the Corsican usurper Napoleon Bonaparte. Having made himself "First Consul" on the day still remembered as 18 Brumaire 1799, the new military dictator waited only a short time to declare that the French revolution was, after ten tempestuous years, at an end. This "Proclamation" was issued on December 15, 1799. On the preceding day, George Washington had died. No two moments, separately or in combination, could have given Americans a stronger sense of an impending new century.

If Washington's resignation as president had opened the fissure between competing factions, his death was to disclose deep divisions within his own party of Federalism. And the chief of these divisions also concerned relations with France. Dr. George Logan, a well-meaning Quaker, had embarked on a mission to Paris to see if the "quasi-war" might not be replaced with a treaty. (His name survives in today's Logan Act, passed by irascible Federalists to outlaw private diplomacy by unaccredited American citizens.) He returned with plausible evidence that there was goodwill on the French side, if only because of the shattering defeat of the French navy by Admiral Horatio Nelson, who had destroyed the rear guard of Bonaparte's Egyptian expedition at the mouth of the Nile. Jefferson suddenly found events breaking his way. President Adams was aware that his new taxes for an increased military establishment had become unpopular—at least in the absence of an outright war with France. Hamilton accepted this logic, but demanded just such a war. Adams temporized by sending a new set of negotiators to Paris. Meanwhile, with the advent of an imperialist Napoleon, Jefferson felt himself free of any commitment to the revolutionary or republican French. (In this, he perhaps unconsciously emulated his detested Federalist enemies, who had argued that treaties made with King Louis were void once the monarchy had been deposed by the Jacobins.)

In these favorable circumstances, in which the evidence is that Jefferson himself did not at first believe (he avoided saying anything at all when Washington died), a rancorous quarrel also erupted between his rivals Adams and Hamilton. Adams accused Hamilton of managing a private cabal within the government and dismissed two of those (Secretary of War James McHenry and Secretary of State Timothy Pickering) whom he believed to be part of it. Hamilton replied with a letter which he had not intended to be "open" denouncing Adams and inciting Federalists to support Charles Pinckney—one of the moral heroes of the "XYZ" affair. But that affair and its repercussions were now subject to diminishing returns, and the publication of Hamilton's letter was discrediting both to him and to his presidential target. Suddenly, it was the Federalists who were ridiculed because of "leaks," and also divided in respect of policy toward France.

Concerning the epoch-changing election of 1800, there seems to be no embellishing anecdote about Jefferson's reluctance to place his name in nomination. There appears instead to have been a universal assumption that he would be the Republican candidate. There also appears to have been a high confidence, at first apparently justified, in his victory. When he met President Adams in his official capacity, soon after a Republican victory in the New York legislature, which had been superbly managed by Aaron Burr, Adams said curtly, "Well, I understand that you are to beat me in this contest." His vice president responded soothingly that if both of them were to die, the contest would continue along similar principles and identical lines of division. (This is the period at which Americans began to revere the notion of orderly transitions of power between opposing parties, a thing that was still unknown anywhere else in the world.) Not all participants were so sanguine: realizing that the New York legislature would appoint Republicans to the electoral college—thus leading to "a REVOLUTION, after the manner of BONA-PARTE," who had just led a counterrevolution—Alexander Hamilton pressed Governor John Jay to nullify the result that his future assassin had helped to bring about. His effort was not persuasive.

The acrimony of the 1800 election is best captured by the most inventive of the allegations made against Jefferson. To the usual charges that he was an atheist and an anarchist was added the apparently unanswerable claim that he was dead. This venomous rumor was widely believed, even by some of his supporters. But a headline with the auspicious date of July 4 proclaimed him still among the living. The once-repressed Democratic clubs performed prodigies of campaigning and organization (the actual official name of the ticket was the Democratic-Republican Party), and the outcome appeared at first to be a clean and decisive sweep, with a Republican victory in both houses of Congress and in the contest for both of the top two posts. However, upon examination it proved that Jefferson, campaigning once again with Aaron Burr on his ticket, had received exactly the same number of electoral votes as his running mate. He had been so confident of the result that he wrote to Burr, regretting that appointing him vice president would mean losing him as a member of the cabinet. But Burr replied that he was prepared to wait and see who the president was to be. And this in turn meant that the existing lame-duck House of Representatives, not the newly elected body that was to be seated in 1801, had the job of deciding the issue. Even before this could happen, the electoral ballots had to be counted, state by state, in the Senate. As vice president, Thomas Jefferson presided in the Senate and officiated at this count.

There are numerous versions of what happened next, and why. Professor Bruce Ackerman of Yale and his coauthor David Fontana have pointed out the invidious position in which Jefferson was placed; first when he was confronted with clear evidence that the Georgia ballot had been subject to tampering. He nonetheless awarded the state's eight votes to himself and to Burr. There is no doubt that this was the intention of Georgia's voters, so no actual question of fraud arises, and Jefferson and Burr had in any case won by a margin of larger than four each, but the fact remains that if they had received less than seventy votes apiece they would have had to face a runoff with the other three candidates—Adams, Pinckney, and Jay.

To this head-swimming collision of arithmetic and interest (not really cleared up until the passage of the Twelfth Amendment to the Constitution in 1804, and still a possible anomaly to this day, should there be any question of the validity of any state's ballot) has been added a grave charge by Professor Garry Wills. Jefferson's vote, in this account, was greatly inflated by the ballots cast on behalf of disenfranchised slaves in the south, who were counted under the federal Constitution as "three fifths" of a citizen and carried the same weight in the Electoral College. The "three fifths law" did not apply to the Senate, and the view—of Jefferson's indebtedness to "the slave power" and of his awareness of that indebtedness—may still not justify Professor Wills's enthusiasm for Pinckney. Nonetheless, it may be said to darken the radiant picture of 1801 as a "second revolution," or a new beginning for democratic politics.

In truth, the scene in the House in February of 1801 was something less than edifying. Many if not most Republicans had merely assumed that Burr was only competing for the vice presidency, and many on this basis had voted for him as a way of canceling the hurt inflicted by his poor showing (particularly in the South) in 1796. But Burr possessed an odd combination of qualities. A grandson of the fiery Calvinist sermonizer Jonathan Edwards, he was a man with a distinguished record in combat and a hero in the bedroom and boardroom to boot, with many lucrative speculations to his credit. He was well able to make friends, and enemies, for life. One of the more determined enemies was his fellow New Yorker and future victim Alexander Hamilton. Indeed, and to his credit, Hamilton quite swallowed his detestation of Jefferson in his loathing for Burr. A number of other Federalists joined Hamilton in believing that Burr's election would be a calamity. After no fewer than thirty-five deadlocked ballots in the House, the tie was eventually broken on the initiative of James Bayard of Delaware. His state, along with South Carolina, abandoned Burr by casting a blank ballot, while Vermont and Maryland abstained. Thus on the thirty-sixth ballot, on February 17, 1801, Thomas Jefferson was chosen to be the third president of the United States.

Some Federalists continued to act with bad grace. John Adams, the first incumbent president to be defeated, left the new capital of Washington before his successor could be inaugurated. He had, perhaps, the excuse of a bereavement with the recent loss of his son Charles. Alexander Hamilton, however, proposed that from then on presidential electors should cast separate ballots for the presidency and the vice presidency (this was the scheme later adopted as the Twelfth Amendment). Jefferson resolved to speak in the spirit of reconciliation, and on March 4, 1801, delivered—almost inaudibly, as was his wont—an inaugural speech that gratified most of those who heard, or rather read it:

> Every difference of opinion is not a difference of principle. We have called by different names brethren of the same principle. We are all republicans, we are all federalists. If there be any among us who would wish to dissolve this Union or to change its republican form, let them stand undisturbed as monuments of the safety with which error of opinion may be tolerated where reason is left free to combat it.

That passage, with its implied rebuke to the spirit and letter of the Alien and Sedition Acts, seems to be a conscious echo of Milton's *Areopagitica*, one of the greatest essays of the English Revolution: "And though all the winds of doctrine were let loose to play upon the earth, so truth be in the field, we do injuriously by licensing and prohibiting to misdoubt her strength. Let her and falsehood grapple; who ever knew truth put to the worst, in a free and open encounter?" Testifying to faith in a democratic and patriotic citizenry, Jefferson went on to speak of a government where

> every man, at the call of the law, would fly to the standard of the law, and would meet invasions of the public order as his own personal concern. Sometimes it is said that man cannot be trusted with the government of himself. Can he then be

trusted with the government of others? Or have we found angels in the form of kings to govern him? Let history answer this question.

The other moment of significance in the speech was Jefferson's declaration that while America would seek amicable relations with all nations it would embark on "entangling alliances with none." This was his coded farewell to the French, and an expression of his determination that the United States should become a power in its own right. A new capital city, in Washington, a new century, a new president and—who was to say?—perhaps a new epoch, too.

Chapter Seven

Mr. President

IT MAY STILL BE argued that Jefferson was a Dixiecrat *avant la lettre*, and the imposing nature of history makes it near impossible to imagine what would have eventuated if Adams or Burr had won the election of 1800–1801, but the record as it comes down to us makes it possible to state that without Thomas Jefferson as president, it is in the highest degree improbable that the United States would exist as we know it today, or even as we knew it a century ago.

There were three particular and nation-building chapters to Jefferson's time in office: the Barbary Wars, the Louisiana Purchase, and the Lewis and Clark expedition to the West. All three of them testify to Jefferson's astonishing single-mindedness (as well as to his reluctance to forget a slight), and all three of them originate partly with his time in Paris. It will be simpler to consider them first as self-contained, and then as inter-connected.

Between the years 1530 and 1780, it has been calculated by the historian Robert Davis, as many as a million and a quarter Europeans were kidnapped and enslaved by Muslim autocracies on the northwest coast of Africa. This trade, which combined piracy, ransom, and enforced servitude, was not the equal of the infamous Middle Passage in which so many bartered black Africans lost their lives, nor was it as organized and commercialized as the "triangular" trade in slaves that flourished between Europe, Africa, and the Americas. But it did in some ways result from that trade, too, in that European interlopers had disrupted an earlier North African Arab involvement in a north-south transport of African slaves. Many well-authenticated chronicles of the period tell of "Barbary" raids on coastal towns as far away as England and Ireland, as well as numberless abductions from, and of, vessels in the Mediterranean and other seaways. It appears, for example, that practically every inhabitant of the Irish village of Baltimore was carried off in 1631. Samuel Pepys and Daniel Defoe both allude to the trade in their writings, Robinson Crusoe himself spending some hard time as a captured slave. James Thomson's famous 1740 popular song "Rule Britannia," with its refrain about Britons "never, never, never" being slaves, was composed with the Barbary terror in mind.

It was the general policy of European powers to make their separate peaces with the rulers of Algiers, Morocco, Tripoli, and Tunis (and it had also been the policy of some of them to take Muslim slaves when they could, as well as to vary the business with an occasional punitive expedition). By the time of the American Revolution, however, the rule in most European capitals was to pay a given amount of tribute to the "Barbary" powers—so-called partly because of their original Berber population, and also because of the handy euphony of the word with barbarism—in exchange either for redeemed captives or for a wider immunity from plunder and kidnap. It was reckoned as part of the cost of doing business. It could also be useful, in secret dealings with one or another emir or sultan, to cut out a competitor nation.

The new United States could hardly approach this with equanimity. It did not have a navy with which to protect its commercial ships, or with which to threaten retaliation. Its trade had declined, in fact, as a result of having lost such protection from the British Empire. Moreover, vengeful elements in London were not above encouraging the North Africans to pick off American ships and thereby teach the seceding colonists a lesson.

During the time that he and John Adams were, respectively, the United States ministers to Paris and London, Thomas Jefferson conceived a great loathing for this state of affairs. In 1784 the American ship *Betsey*, with a crew of ten, had been taken by a Moroccan corsair while sailing with a cargo of salt from Cádiz, in southern Spain, to Philadelphia. Not long afterward, Algerian ships had seized the *Dauphin* and the *Maria* in the Atlantic. From his post in New York, Secretary of State John Jay had instructed his two American envoys to follow the European example and make treaties with the abductors. They were authorized to borrow large sums of money from Dutch bankers for the purpose of paying tribute.

Seeking clarification, Adams invited Jefferson to London for a private meeting with the ambassador of Tripoli. On this occasion, Ambassador Abdrahaman mentioned some startlingly high tariffs for ransom of hostages, for cheap terms of "temporary peace," and for more costly terms of "perpetual peace," not forgetting to add his own personal commission on the negotiation. Since the United States had not offended the Muslim powers in any way—it had not taken part in the Crusades, for example, or the Spanish monarchy's reconquest of Andalusia—Adams and Jefferson asked to know by what right this levy was being exacted. As Jefferson later wrote, to Jay and to Congress, on March 28, 1786:

> The Ambassador answered us that it was founded on the Laws of the Prophet, that it was written in their Koran, that all nations who should not have answered their authority were sinners, that it was their right and duty to make war upon them wherever they could be found, and to make slaves of all they could take as prisoners.

It is hard to imagine a better summary of all that Jefferson disliked, both about monarchy and religion, but he did not dilate on this point, preferring to recommend to the administration that it refuse all payment of tribute, and prepare at once to outfit an American naval squadron to visit the Mediterranean. In the longer run, he wrote, what was needed was an international concert of powers, composed of all those nations whose shipping was being subjected to predatory raids. "Justice and Honor favor this course," he wrote, not omitting to add that it would also save money in the end.

John Adams was not at all of the same opinion. He agreed that "Avarice and Fear are the only agents at Algiers," and that "it would be a good occasion to begin a navy," but he was certain that Congress would never appropriate the money for a punitive expedition, and meanwhile the United States had no navy to speak of. "From these premises I conclude it to be wisest for us to negotiate and pay the necessary sum without loss of time." As for the piratical Islamic powers, "We ought not to fight them at all unless we determine to fight them forever." In my view, Jefferson's opinion of Adams began to decline from that point. But as the junior, he made a formal bow to the apparent wisdom of such a policy.

Privately, however, he had long before made up his mind that there would be a reckoning with the Barbary corsairs. In the paragraph on the slave trade that was struck out of his first draft of the Declaration of Independence, he had referred caustically to the way in which the "Christian king of Great Britain" was engaging in "this piratical warfare, the opprobrium of infidel powers." This seems to me to be a clear allusion to the Barbary practices. In November 1784, long before the meeting with Abdrahaman, he had written to James Madison, "We ought to begin a naval power, if we mean to carry on our own commerce. Can we begin it on a more honourable occasion or with a weaker foe? I am of opinion [John] Paul Jones with half a dozen frigates would totally destroy their commerce." Later, while in Paris, he had begun an association with John Paul Jones, seafaring hero of the American Revolution and often described as the founder of the United States Navy. The relationship seems to have begun with Jefferson acting as a go-between for Jones and his then-current mistress, Madame Townsend. She was the widow of an Englishman and the reputed illegitimate daughter of King Louis XV. We only know her identity by way of Jefferson's papers: he seems to have performed his intermediary role with some skill (further proof of his worldliness in matters sexual), but appears to have stopped short of obliging her when she solicited a loan. In late 1787, Jefferson made a proposition of quite a different kind to Jones. Through diplomatic channels, he had heard that the Empress Catherine ("the Great") of Russia would like to hire the naval hero as the head of a fleet, with the express purpose of driving the Turks out of the Black Sea.

Jones was at the time in very low water, financially and emotionally, and was inclined to take the job. But why was Jefferson offering it to him? Jones's biographer speculates that Jefferson wanted to keep Jones actively employed, and acquiring new battle experience, until America could build its own fleet. I think that Jefferson was also interested in Jones's prospective enemy. Three of the four Barbary states—Algiers, Tripoli, and Tunis—were part of the Ottoman Empire. Britain, a Protestant power, held three important naval bases on the fringes of Catholic Europe, at Gibraltar, Minorca, and Malta. It employed trade-offs with Turkey and the Barbary states to help balance its sea power. Why, then, should not America, in return, discreetly help Russia to make life difficult for the Turks?

Jones set off for Saint Petersburg in May of 1788, keeping Jefferson informed by correspondence. He met Empress Catherine, and presented her with a copy of the newly promulgated United States Constitution. His years in Russia were to prove extremely arduous, because he became involved in the vicious intrigues of the empress's court, but he did see some considerable service in the Black Sea and managed to inflict some hard blows on the Turkish navy. He proposed, it seems on his own initiative, an alliance between the United States and Russia against the Mediterranean pirates. He also argued for "going to the source" and leading a Russian squadron into the Mediterranean to attack Ottoman shipping between Constantinople and Egypt. For these and other impertinences on the side of the infidels, he had a price put on his head by the Dey of Algiers.

Eventually undermined in Russia by his rivals, out of favor with the empress, and suffering from jaundice and nephritis, Jones made his way back to Paris and died in lonely and sordid circumstances in July 1792. By this time, Jefferson had been replaced as minister in Paris by Gouverneur Morris, who was as disgusted and annoyed at having to deal with Jones's effects as he had been at having to cope with the imprisoned Thomas Paine. A packet arrived from the State Department addressed to Jones, just after his death. It contained an invitation from Jefferson. He had wanted Jones to lead a delegation to Algiers, threatening the Dey with serious consequences if his policy of extortion continued, and he had persuaded George Washington to sign a commission for Jones to this effect.

In 1793, Jefferson retired as secretary of state. But the Barbary question had by then taken on a life of its own. The dismal plight of American hostages in North African jails—the subject of several of Jones's letters to Jefferson—had become a serious issue in the United States. Not only was their treatment appallingly cruel, but they were threatened with forcible conversion to Islam and—it was rumored—with sexual practices too revolting to describe. Their piteous letters from prison stirred a large public agitation that eventually compelled Congress, in 1794, to commission six frigates for the Barbary shore. Three of these—the *United States*, the *Constitution,* and the *Constellation*—were actually built. America was beginning to have a permanent navy even if, by a historical irony and contradiction, it was most often the Jeffersonian Republicans who opposed the expense of such a force, as well as the violation it implied of the cherished prohibition on standing armies. But as on previous occasions, Jefferson himself had been separated from the immediate political scuffle and was in "retirement" at Monticello, busily expanding his library. Having sent his message to Congress in 1790, entitled "Proposal to Use Force Against the Barbary States," he had willed the end while leaving the means to others. And in his absence, his pet cause acquired merit by association. It benefited from an increase in federal revenues (including those raised by the much reviled whiskey tax), and it benefited from Federalist hostility to France during the "quasi-war" with French privateers. Thus when James Madison rose to speak against the large new naval appropriations of 1794, the moral leader of his Republican faction, secure in Virginia, was able to preserve a sphinx-like silence. When the "XYZ" affair exploded four years later, spurring fresh calls for rearmament and against "tribute," Vice President Jefferson was able to do as he had done with the Genet fiasco and balance outrage against France with continuing resentment of Britain's hidden hand in the Mediterranean. By the time he assumed the presidency, he was in command not just of a new navy, well built by John Adams, but also of the United States Marine Corps, created in July 1798.

Jefferson's long-meditated ruthlessness against the Barbary powers—he even proposed capturing their sailors in retaliation and selling them at the large Christian-run slave market in Malta—was given every opportunity to vent itself by the greed and stupidity of the pashas. Yusuf Karamanli, the ruler of Tripoli, had been rash enough to issue an ultimatum to the United States in late 1800, threatening war if his exorbitant conditions were not met. In effect, President Jefferson coolly decided to take this latent declaration of war at face value. He secured agreement from his cabinet on the dispatch of a squadron, and further determined not to trouble Congress with the matter. Its members were in recess anyway, but surely the president in time of war had the authority to act alone? Only three months after his inauguration, the squadron was on the high seas, and Jefferson did not inform Congress until the warships had sailed far enough to be effectively beyond recall. Over the next four years, the Barbary coast was effectively "pacified" by a unilateral American expedition, laconically described by the president as a continuous "cruise." Under bombardment or the threat of it, Algeria, Morocco, and Tunis gradually ceased their cooperation with the pasha of Tripoli. Yusuf, however, remained intransigent, even daring to board and capture the USS *Philadelphia* in 1803.

When he came to write his magnificent study of the Jefferson administrations, Henry Adams was old enough, and had once been young enough, to celebrate the names of the American heroes whose exploits had been the stuff of his boyhood reading. Two episodes in particular, culminating the victory of American arms, are still remembered. In February of 1804 Captain Stephen Decatur sailed right into Tripoli harbor. The captured *Philadelphia* was put to the torch rather than let it remain in Barbary hands. That August, Decatur returned, bombarding the fortified town, boarding the pasha's own fleet where it lay at anchor, and rescuing the *Philadelphia*'s crew from a gruesome imprisonment. According to legend, and to some eyewitnesses, Decatur slew the very Muslim warrior who had earlier killed his brother, Lieutenant James Decatur. The following year, in April of 1805, young Captain William Eaton led a mixed force of Arabs, mercenaries, and American marines on a desert march from inland that captured Derna, the second city of Tripoli (today's Libya). Lieutenant Presley O'Bannon raised the Stars and Stripes over the vanquished town, marking the first occasion that the American flag had been planted in battle on a foreign shore. This moment is preserved in the opening line of the Marine anthem, which begins, "From the halls of Montezuma to the shores of Tripoli."

Coming as they did so soon after the Louisiana Purchase, these victories and their high cost in money (as well as the war's "presidential" and somewhat secretive character) aroused some Federalist criticism. But there was, in effect, no arguing with success. It took a little while longer for all the Barbary states to sign treaties with the United States, renouncing piracy and kidnapping. There was an awkward moment in Washington when the Tunisian envoy, Sidi Soliman Melli Melli, expected to be amused at the public expense with the company of some ladies of the night. (Jefferson and Madison, once again demonstrating familiarity with the facts of life, arranged an off-the-record State Department fund for this express purpose.) Further punitive expeditions against Algiers were required in the coming years, but in essence Jefferson's policy was an unalloyed triumph for peace, and the freedom of trade from blackmail, through the exercise of planned force. The reputation of the United States was considerably enhanced, and Decatur's battle-tested navy was to prove itself in even sterner combat in the war of 1812.

The Louisiana Purchase

It might be agreeable to attribute Jefferson's success in North Africa to a general policy of using American force on the side of tyranny and against slavery, but any comparison with Santo Domingo/Haiti would weaken if not fatally destroy such a claim. In correspondence, indeed, Jefferson referred to a slave-ruled Haiti as potentially "another Algiers in the seas of America," an especially strong mode of condemnation, though not as downright rough as his allusion to "the Cannibals of the terrible republic."

Having had no real say in Haitian affairs since quitting his post as secretary of state in 1793, Jefferson had not at all relaxed his hostility to, and fear of, the slave rebellion. The Adams administration had, without Jefferson's approval or involvement, been fairly friendly to the idea of Haitian independence from France. This reflected both the antislavery emphasis of at least some of the Federalist New Englanders, such as Secretary of State Timothy Pickering, and their embittered hostility to the French. Jefferson's policy as president was rather different. He supported French efforts to regain control of Haiti—with the implication that this would lead to the restoration of slavery—not just because he disliked slave revolts but because he hoped that the large American commerce with the island, and the rest of the Caribbean basin, would thereby expand.

One might observe here that Jefferson was being untrue even to his professed principles on matters of slavery and color. He had proposed the emancipation of American slaves, followed by their expatriation to Africa or the West Indies. This scheme, commonly known as "colonization," depended on there being some nearby black-ruled territory where the slaves could go, or be sent. Yet when it came to it, Jefferson denied the right of Haitians to establish such a state. One of his most caustic critics, the historian Michael Zuckerman, drew on the metaphor of Exodus and extremely chillingly summarized Jefferson's attitude to the slaves: "Even as he yearned to get rid of them, he refused to let them go."

But Napoleon's termination of the French Revolution also allowed Jefferson to be much more pragmatic as between France and England. In his first conversation with the French envoy Louis

Pichon in July 1801, he even proposed that the two warring countries make peace together and jointly restore order in the Caribbean. He certainly gave the impression, to Napoleon and his foreign minister Talleyrand, that American support would be available to France in any event. This assurance was important to the French, and had recently become more so. In Haiti itself an unprecedented thing had occurred. A brilliant rebel general, perhaps the first slave leader since the possibly mythical Spartacus, had emerged in the person of Toussaint L'Ouverture. Massing the slaves behind him in a formidable army, Toussaint had proclaimed the first black-ruled republic in history. Napoleon, who was not at all interested in peace with England, hoped by a decisive action to restore French power in the transatlantic region and thereby raise new money for his even wider imperial design. He dispatched an army and a fleet to Haiti, under the command of General Leclerc, in October of 1801.

The story of that expedition's defeat and near annihilation at the hands of a slave phalanx has been compellingly told in C. L. R. James's masterpiece *The Black Jacobins*. The French army and navy were destroyed, in effect, by the ideas of the French revolution (with some help, admittedly, from disease). Eventually, Toussaint was captured, transported to France, imprisoned in a freezing cell in the French Pyrenees and allowed to die from callous neglect. But in the meantime, Napoleon's hope for a renewed French dominion in the region had been sunk. And his ruined armies and ships in Haiti had never received the American support and sympathy that they had been expecting.

Though they are generally oblivious on the point, Americans

have good reason to be grateful for the exertions of Toussaint and his heroic rebels. Without them, the United States might never have gained control of the Mississippi and the Midwest. One can almost suspect Jefferson of seeing this opportunity coming, and at the very least of doing nothing to postpone it. And once again, we have evidence of his long-term single-mindedness. In 1786 he had put it like this:

> Our confederacy must be viewed as the nest from which all America, North and South, is to be peopled. We should take care not to think for the interest of that great continent [South America, with the isthmus and islands] to press too soon on the Spaniards. Those countries cannot be in better hands. My fear is that they are too feeble to hold them till our population can be sufficiently advanced to gain it from them piece by piece. The navigation of the Mississippi we must have. This is all we are as yet ready to receive.

In his mind, Jefferson saw a future America that extended down through Florida at least as far as Cuba, and then from west of the Mississippi as far as it could go. This outcome depended on two things—the dexterous management of rivalries between England, France, and Spain, and the birth of enough people to furnish settlers in the new lands.

The main contiguous power along the Mississippi and at New Orleans, in the first years of the nineteenth century, was Spain. This

suited Jefferson in general, because Spain was weak and might be
dealt with at leisure. But it did pose the danger of new American settlements asking for Spanish protection and stunting the expansion
of the Union. Spain and France had alternated as allies and enemies
during the war years, and in 1803 Jefferson was alarmed to learn that
by a new alliance Bonaparte had taken over all the Spanish posses-
sions in the Southeast, including New Orleans and Louisiana. This
move was more theoretical than practical, since France's huge reverse
in Haiti meant that it was in no serious position to reinforce or gar-
rison the mouth of the Mississippi. Swiftly apprehending the significance of this gulf between theory and practice, Jefferson sent his
friend Robert Livingston to Paris to inquire whether Talleyrand and
Napoleon might be induced to sell New Orleans at the right price.
Talleyrand—one of the profiteers in the "XYZ" affair—at first
seemed to decline. Jefferson sent James Monroe to upgrade the delegation, and wrote a letter to his negotiators that he wished them to
allow Napoleon and Talleyrand to see:

There is on the globe one single spot, the possessor of which
is our natural and habitual enemy. It is New Orleans, through
which the produce of three-eighths of our territory must pass
to market, and from its fertility it will ere long yield more
than half of our whole produce and contain more than half
our inhabitants. . . . The day that France takes possession of
New Orleans fixes the sentence which is to restrain her forever within her low-water mark. It seals the union of two na-

tions who in conjunction can maintain exclusive possession of the ocean. *From that moment we must marry ourselves to the British fleet and nation.* [Emphasis added.]

As with the case of the Barbary states, Jefferson plainly thought that the American imperative itself had been meditated and rehearsed long enough, and that the hour for pitiless decision had arrived. It is not absolutely clear whether or not the French quite believed in his threat of an alliance with Britain, but it is safe to say that both Napoleon and Talleyrand, for perhaps different reasons, had an urgent need for immediate gold, in order to prosecute their wars against Great Britain and Russia. Even before Monroe could take his place at the bargaining table to barter over the original offer of ten million dollars for New Orleans, the French side came back to Livingston with another proposal. Fifteen million dollars would purchase all of the American territory that France had to sell: an extent of land so much larger than Louisiana that its true size was unknown. (When Livingston asked Talleyrand how much territory was involved, he received the shrugging reply, "I can give you no direction. You have made a noble bargain for yourselves, and I suppose you will make the most of it." What a perfect revenge for the attempted extortions of the XYZ team.) The best computation to be made at the time was that the United States had approximately doubled its area of sovereignty, at a cost of four cents an acre. Henry Adams phrased it with his usual pith:

The annexation of Louisiana was an event so portentous as to defy measurement; it gave a new face to politics, and ranked in historical importance next to the Declaration of Independence and the adoption of the Constitution—events of which it was the logical outcome; but as a matter of diplomacy it was unparalleled, because it cost almost nothing.

In point of fact, it was far from certain that such a momentous secret negotiation was at all the "logical outcome" of the adoption of the Constitution. Jefferson confronted this ticklish question with a characteristic mixture of pedantry and elasticity. At first he gave the Constitution a close reading, but failed to discover any formulation that would permit the federal government to acquire fresh national territory, or to spend the necessary money, without authorization. (He must have remembered, either with annoyance or embarrassment, his firm statement that the Constitution did not even allow Alexander Hamilton to establish a national bank.) At one stage, he went as far as drafting a constitutional amendment that would meet the case, telling one senator from Virginia:

> When an instrument admits two constructions, the one safe, the other dangerous, the one precise, the other indefinite, I prefer that which is safe and precise. I had rather ask an enlargement of power from the nation, where it is found necessary, than to assume it by a construction which would make our powers boundless. Our peculiar security is in possession

of a written constitution. Let us not make it a blank paper by construction. . . . Let us go on then perfecting it, by adding, by way of amendment to the Constitution, those powers which time and trial show are still wanting.

However, there came two rumors that forced Jefferson's hand and compelled his abrupt abandonment of niceties about the Constitution. It was said that Napoleon was reconsidering the wisdom of the bargain he had made, and it was also understood that the Spanish authorities might contest the basis of the proposed deal, on the argument that nobody had delineated the proper boundaries of Louisiana. Jefferson had already decided that the Spanish-owned Florida territories could be added to the acquisition in good time, and that even though Madrid would not sell now, then if "as soon as she is at war, we push them strongly with one hand, holding out a price with the other, we shall certainly obtain the Floridas." This prophecy was later to be vindicated by General Andrew Jackson; it remained meanwhile to secure the signature of France, and of the United States Senate, on what had been gained in Paris. Thus Jefferson switched, almost without taking a breath, to the view that "the less that is said about my constitutional difficulty, the better; and that it will be desirable for Congress to do what is necessary *in silence*."

He assumed that there would be immense public sympathy for a stroke of national aggrandizement as bold as this one. He also imagined that it would put the Federalists very much upon the defensive. He was correct on both counts. The sheer scale and daring of the enterprise commanded general support, and the Senate gave him an overwhelming majority after an almost perfunctory debate. When the treaty was signed, Robert Livingston probably spoke for a majority in saying, "From this day, the United States take their place among the powers of first rank." (Pause to note the locution: it was not until after Gettysburg that Americans began to say "the United States is" rather than "the United States are.") Meanwhile, Alexander Hamilton sarcastically commented that the Purchase should be attributed to "the kind interpositions of an overruling Providence," while much of the New England Federalist press suddenly became strictly and literally constructionist, and ridiculed the bargain as an exchange of precious cold cash, of which the United States had too little, for land, of which it already had too much. On the constitutional point, John Quincy Adams was even more eloquent. He asserted that the president would now dispose of "an assumption of implied power greater . . . than all of the assumptions of implied power in the years of the Washington and Adams administrations put together." This criticism, as Jefferson contentedly understood, had the merit of being true.

He proposed to govern the new territory, at least at first, by an appointed governor and an unelected "Assembly of Notables." In his letters, he referred to his new subjects in precisely the terms that have always been employed by imperial proconsuls—which is to say, he described them as "children" who needed to be guided to maturity. (In a moment that perhaps indicated his bad conscience on this point, he asked the Marquis de Lafayette, who was at least a French reformer with democratic sympathies, to take on the job of Louisiana's governorship.)

The administrative and constitutional issues paled when set against the critical matter that dogged every step of Jefferson's career. Having secured New Orleans and the Mississippi by the rather unsentimental expedient of betraying the revolution in Haiti as well as double-crossing France, he had to answer the question: Would the great sin of slavery be extenuated further by this massive acquisition, or would it at least be attenuated?

This is not one of those questions about slavery that is only asked in retrospect, or by a more easily shocked posterity. It was apparent at the time, and hotly argued. Thomas Paine, who had urged the idea of a Louisiana Purchase upon Jefferson without knowing that he was already engaged in it, begged him to keep slavery out of the new lands and to settle German migrants there instead of black slaves. James Hillhouse of Connecticut, a Federalist congressman, proposed an amendment to the Louisiana legislation protecting the territory from the practice, and was warmly supported by Joel Barlow, who like Paine was one of Jefferson's personal friends. In theory, as well as in morality and law, the case was no different from the prohibition of any extension of slavery that Jefferson himself had proposed in the Northwest ordinance of 1787. However, the interest of sugar prevailed in 1804, just as the interest of cotton would prevail later on. Louisiana might, as Paine had argued, produce more sugar in the long run if it were settled by industrious Germans, but it would produce less sugar in the here-and-now if slavery were done away with, and meanwhile the rival producers in the West Indies would seize the advantage. So the most that the president would concede was a prohibition on the purchase of imported slaves, a step to the abolition of the foreign slave trade itself in January 1808.

Jefferson's crucial and conscious refusal to enlarge the vision of abolition led to the admission of Louisiana itself as a slave state and to the subsequent admission of states formed from the wider territory of the Purchase, so that by 1819 there were twenty-two states of the Union, eleven with slavery and eleven without: exactly the contradiction of "half slave and half free" that was later to trouble Mr. Lincoln. It was to be Missouri, the next state formed from the Louisiana lands, that tipped the balance.

The Lewis and Clark Expedition

Since Jefferson could hardly have been unaware that his Louisiana diplomacy had deeply compromised three of his cherished principles—the abolition of slavery, the vaunted Republican mode of democracy, and the integrity of the Union—it is fair to ask what might have actuated him in taking the risk. The answer is relatively simple. He knew something that neither his Federalist foes nor his Republican allies did. For several years, he had been meditating and preparing an expedition to the West. And it must have given him enormous satisfaction, on the day in July 1803 that he dispatched Lewis and Clark, to be able to tell them that the Indian chiefs they would be meeting now owed their allegiance to a new country. The "uncharted" lands, to an extent that could not have been anticipated, were *already* part of the United States.

Again, the germ of the idea had been present during Jefferson's diplomatic sojourn in Paris, if not, indeed, slightly before. In 1783 he had asked General George Rodgers Clark, a hero of the wars on the frontier, to go as a scout into the West, but the general had declined. Two years later, during his period of service in Paris, Jefferson had learned that King Louis was outfitting an expedition to the Pacific Northwest under the command of Comte La Perouse. Notwithstanding official French claims that the endeavor was purely scientific in character, Jefferson and John Paul Jones concluded that Paris was interested in establishing colonies on the farther shore of the North American continent. The following year, Jefferson held some conversation with a rather bizarre adventurer named John Ledyard, who had sailed with Captain James Cook and had become the first American to visit the Pacific Northwest. Ledyard had formed a quixotic scheme to travel through European Russia, cross Siberia, traverse the Bering Strait, and then walk across the continent to the East Coast and make his report. Jefferson encouraged him in this idea, which did not materialize in the way that Jones's posting to Russia had done. (Empress Catherine arrested and deported Ledyard as soon as he got as far as Siberia.)

But the expedition led by the Comte La Perouse never returned—its wreckage was found decades later on a Pacific island—and so the question of the interior and the West was still open by the time Jefferson became secretary of state. In 1792, he entertained a proposal from the French naturalist André Michaux to explore the origins and outlets of the American river system. However, Michaux in his turn proved to be part naturalist and part agent: his connection with French interests and French espionage brought the exploration to a premature close.

The parallel with French initiative (and the need to preempt it) is suggestive. When contemplating his famous occupation of Egypt toward the end of the nineteenth century, Napoleon Bonaparte summoned all manner of historians, cartographers, botanists, linguists, anthropologists, and architects to smooth his path and enlarge his dominion. Most scholars date the concept of European Orientalism from this grandiose, scholarly, but imperial design. Jefferson knew that Americans would not be confronting any large armies or ancient cities when they moved westward, but he was likewise concerned to make the expedition into a project of learning as well as one of mapping and acquisition. He also wanted an internal market to counterweigh dependence upon the Atlantic Ocean and the capricious powers who still partly dominated it. One might term his scheme an "Occidentalist" one.

At the back of his mind, also, was the inescapable question of the tobacco-and-slave economy upon which his own status depended, and which he semi-consciously understood to be doomed. The colonial economy was rich in land and poor in cash—Hamilton had been technically right on this point—and it was furthermore labor-intensive while starved for capital. The "small tobacco" system was agriculturally wasteful and promiscuous, draining goodness from the soil in pursuit of a short-term crop. Longer-term management, involving crop rotation and soil husbandry, would have meant less short-term revenue. Jefferson had half-confronted this dilemma in his *Notes on the State of Virginia*, writing in a rare concession to European superiority, that American agricultural inferiority resulted "from our having such quantities of land to waste as we please. In Europe the object is to make the most of their land, labor being abundant; here it is to make the most of our labor, land being abundant."

Like a number of those who split the moral difference on slavery as it occurred in everyday politics, Jefferson (like his Monticello estate, land-rich and cash-poor) justified himself by the belief that a younger generation would cleanse the inherited stain, and that the expansion of America would "diffuse" the slave system until it shrank and died out of its own accord. This combination of idealism and cynicism is to be found throughout the Lewis and Clark story. Stephen Ambrose has mordantly pointed out that when Jefferson actually met and trained young Virginians and Kentuckians, such as Meriwether Lewis or William Clark (the younger brother of General George Rodgers Clark), he still made no attempt to persuade them of the virtues of emancipation.

The work of discovery, in any case, took precedence. The terms of the Louisiana Purchase were necessarily vague, because nobody knew how far northward the putative Missouri boundary really extended. This gave a sort of carte blanche to Jefferson. But, as with the Purchase itself, he did not feel able to disclose his ambitions to Congress in advance. Funds would be required, but would probably not be forthcoming if proposed for another "botanizing expedition." The noble lie that the president proposed to tell the legislative branch was again based upon an advantage he drew from losing his earlier contest with Hamilton: the Constitution did indeed allow the financing of an expedition devoted to the expansion of commerce. In view of the large trade in furs conducted in the interior, it was not difficult for the president to engage the attention of numerous congressmen. Possibly certain of this in advance, he mixed in some truth with his deception and declared, "The interests of commerce place the principal object within the constitutional powers and cares of Congress, and that it should incidentally advance the geographical knowledge of our own continent cannot but be an additional gratification." By this cajolery he wrung from Congress the grand sum of two thousand, five hundred dollars for the most momentous exploration in modern history.

In 1940, the first full year of his expatriation in the United States, W. H. Auden wrote a long and beautiful poem to which he gave the name "New Year Letter." In it, he celebrated the immensity and freedom of America as compared to the misery and staleness of Old Europe. He wrote of:

> That culture that had worshipped no
> Virgin before the Dynamo,
> Held no Nicaea or Canossa
> *Hat keine verfallenen Schlösser,*
> *Keine Basalte,* the great Rome
> To all who lost or hated home.

The lines in German, which say that America has "no ruined castles, no marble columns" are taken from a poem by Goethe that opens *"Amerika, du hast es besser"* (America, you have it better).

Auden had also clearly been reading Henry Adams, who wrote at length about the tension between the Virgin and the dynamo in his essays on Europe and America.

The widespread sense of America as a new Eden or virgin land, with a new creation of plants and animals waiting to be discovered, was to some extent qualified by the knowledge that the human species was already present. For many of the advancing or encroaching white settlers, this was nothing more than a noxious problem. And for many of the aboriginal peoples, who had no means of knowing what a dynamo engine of productivity and innovation was beginning to revolve on an eastern seaboard they had never seen, the arrival of white interlopers was no more than another tribal rivalry to be settled by traditional methods.

Mention of these methods also returns us to what Jefferson had written in 1776. In the paragraph immediately preceding the famous (and famously dropped) paragraph on slavery, he accused King George in the following terms:

He has excited domestic insurrection among us, and has endeavored to bring on the inhabitants of our frontiers, the merciless Indian savages, whose known rule of warfare is an undistinguished destruction of all ages, sexes and conditions.

In an earlier pamphlet, as so often, Thomas Paine phrased it better:

These inoffensive people are brought into slavery, by stealing them, tempting kings to sell subjects, which they can have no right to do, and hiring one tribe against another, in order to catch prisoners . . . an height of outrage that seems left by Heathen nations to be practiced by pretended Christians. . . . That barbarous and hellish power which has stirred up the Indians and Negroes to destroy us: the cruelty hath a double guilt—it is dealing brutally by us and treacherously by them.

Notwithstanding the harsh words he had employed while framing the Declaration, Jefferson became anxious to conciliate the Indian peoples. And it is pleasant to record that in this case, at least, he evinced none of the racism, or race theory, that was so prevalent at the time. The racism was that of contemptuous and sometimes terrified white settlers: the race theory was again that of Buffon and his co-thinkers, who thought the native Americans to be good for nothing. Jefferson, by contrast, held that the red of skin were in all respects the natural equal of the white. All that was necessary was for them to learn some agriculture, relieve their women from drudgery, intermarry with Europeans and throw off the pernicious doctrines of their priests, or shamans, and witch doctors.

He established a special room at Monticello for the collection and study of Indian cultural artifacts, and took a special interest in Indian languages and vocabularies, of which he made an immense collection that has since been lost to us. He proposed that the penalty for killing an Indian should be the same in law as for the murder of a white man. The pleasure he took in being considered the Great White Chief, or Father, and in receiving delegations of lesser chiefs at the White House was the nearest he ever came to indulging any monarchical fancies. In fact, his outfitting of the Lewis and Clark expedition was an inversion of the classical theory of the training of princes. Alexander of Macedon had had Aristotle as his tutor; the Florentine rulers had had Machiavelli. But Lewis and Clark had a president to educate them. It even seems probable that Jefferson taught Meriwether Lewis to read and write, or at least to do so to an acceptable standard.

Few details in this education were overlooked. Lewis was sent off to Philadelphia, headquarters of Jefferson's beloved American Philosophical Society, to meet such outstanding men of science and medicine as Dr. Benjamin Rush. He was introduced to the rudiments of astronomy and navigation, as well as receiving instruction in the natural sciences from Benjamin Barton and Caspar Wistar. He was trained in the Jenner method of inoculation against smallpox, in which Jefferson was a strong believer, and encouraged to spread the idea among the tribes he met. So it's not too much to say that the Lewis and Clark expedition was conceived as an Enlightenment project, directed at the spreading of knowledge as much as the acquisition of knowledge, and of the power which that knowledge would of course confer.

The inexact state of knowledge at the time, and the speculations arising, led to a good deal of partisan ridicule from the Federalist side. Jefferson was portrayed as a crackpot, believing in mythical animals and the existence of giants and monsters. (In fact, he did not entirely disbelieve in some rumors from the interior.) As news of the prodigious scope and variety of the real West began to filter back, however, the Federalists were made to look small, or perhaps better say to look as if they had been thinking small—as they had in the case of Louisiana.

For some time, at least, the nobility of the expansionist and ex ploratory enterprise was preserved. Lewis and Clark met with friendliness and with help, not unmixed with suspicion and obstruc- tion, from several of the Indian peoples they encountered. And some of the tribes or nations accepted Jefferson's offer of coexistence. He seems to have reposed particular confidence in any people whose name began with the initial *C:* Cherokees, Choctaws, Chickasaws, and Creeks, the latter of whom actually petitioned for citizenship, while the Cherokees began to settle down, produce a written lan- guage, and put out a newspaper. This lofty and "improving" moment, which was not without its elements of condescension and paternal- ism on the white side, is now perforce viewed by us through the reverse optic of later nightmares and butcheries. The idea of assimilation gave way very fast to its always implied and no less Jeffersonian alternative—that of "Indian removal," in the base euphemism of the time. There are some who say that the suicide of Meriwether Lewis in 1809, brought on by a lethal combination of alcohol, snuff, and manic despair, was the last moment at which the slide from the Jef- fersonian to the Jacksonian could have been prevented. (Lewis's pres- tige, in other words, might have helped arrest it.)

So, Thomas Jefferson doubled the size of the United States and laid out the blueprint upon which it would eventually complete itself as a bicoastal and continental power. (His talks with Ledyard in Paris about the Bering Strait even prefigure Seward's later acquisition of Alaska.) But in even the medium term, his policies also extended and prolonged the "peculiar institution" of slavery, exposed native Americans to rapid and harsh encroachment, and, with his ambitions in the Caribbean and beyond, curtain-raised the seductive ideas of "manifest destiny" and colonial expansion.

Chapter Eight

Disappointment:
The Second Term

I N SOME RESPECTS, the success of Jefferson's first administration was a flaunting of the medals of his earlier defeats. He made use of Hamilton's banking system, of Adams's military and naval strength, of the once-detested Atlantic alliance with Britain and even—in one prosecution of a Federalist editor in New York named Harry Crosswell—the principle of the Alien and Sedition Acts. Some would term this opportunism, not without justice. His defenders might prefer to say that he learned from his mistakes. He certainly knew how to profit from the mistakes of others, and remained very capable of holding a fixed idea and patiently awaiting the moment of vindication.

At the disastrous meeting between King George III and Jefferson and Adams in 1786, it is certain that the Hanoverian monarch did not foresee a time when this upstart ex-colonist from Virginia would be the president of a powerful country. It is not certain that he would have been any more polite if he had been able to imagine such a contingency. At any rate, his rudeness on that occasion—"the ulcerations in the narrow mind of that mulish being," in Jefferson's words—was to rankle for years.

The man upon whom the delayed riposte fell was Anthony Merry, the British envoy to Washington. He arrived to present his credentials, after a lapse in relations between the two countries, in November 1803. It would take the more novelistic pen of a Henry Adams to describe the exquisite social torments that were arranged for him, and the damage done to Anglo-American relations as a consequence. The Merrys (the ambassador's lady was not to be spared) at first found great difficulty in securing decent housing or staff, in a capital that was dank and provincial even by less snobbish standards than theirs. When Merry went to call on Jefferson, accompanied by James Madison, he at first found the official reception room to be bare. Taken down the hallway to the study and introduced informally, Merry declined to believe that he was the victim of any accidental casualness:

> I, in my official costume, found myself at the hour of reception he had himself appointed, introduced to a man as president of the United States, not merely in undress, but *actually standing in slippers down at the heels* [emphasis in original], and both pantaloons, coat and under-clothes indicative of utter slovenliness and indifference to appearances.

This was a mere undress-rehearsal for the dinner party that Thomas Jefferson threw a few nights later. The Merrys arrived at the White House, under the impression that the affair was being held in their honor. They might possibly have overlooked the annoying presence of the French *chargé* Louis Pichon, envoy of an enemy power. They might, with great effort, have forgiven the way that Jefferson allowed his guests to take their seats at dinner randomly, without regard to precedence or seniority. These things actually were routine at presidential soirees. But when Jefferson gave his arm to Dolley Madison—over her own protests—and led her in to dinner leaving Mrs. Merry to make what shift she could, they had no choice but to put the worst interpretation on things. Any lingering doubts on this score were dispelled when Jerome Bonaparte, youngest brother of Napoleon, visited Washington a short while later to show off his dazzling American bride, Elizabeth Patterson. Jefferson gallantly offered his arm to this lady when dinner was served.

On New Year's Day 1804, an already seething Merry paid another courtesy call on the White House, to discover Jefferson deep in conversation with some visiting Indian chieftains. He barely broke off this exchange to acknowledge his British guest, whereupon Merry, protesting that "painted savages" were being preferred to a representative of His Britannic Majesty, stormed out. He would have been yet more incensed if he had ever discovered the low opinion of his wife that Jefferson expressed in a letter to James Monroe, then American minister in London. (She had, he wrote, "established a degree of dislike among all classes which one would have thought impossible in so short a time.")

There were certain implications of historical importance to the playing-out of this grudge match when, later in 1804, Merry had the opportunity for revenge and did seize it with some gusto. In a remarkable episode that still divides historians, he was approached by none other than Jefferson's vice president, Aaron Burr. This inveterate old rake and opportunist had continued to preside coolly over the Senate, in spite of the opprobrium—and the legal indictments from two states—that had fallen upon him after his slaying of Alexander Hamilton in a duel that July. ("I never indeed thought of him as an honest, frank-dealing man," Jefferson was later to remark of Burr, his two-time—and two-timing—running mate, "but considered him as a crooked gun or other perverted machine, whose aim you could never be sure of." The ill-chosen metaphor of Burr's accuracy as a marksman seems doubly unfortunate; ever since the "botanizing excursion" however, he had been politically useful.) His official prospects and his usefulness were now at an end: his party dropped him from the ticket in the 1804 reelection campaign, which Jefferson won easily with Governor George Clinton as running mate.

Foreseeing his inevitable redundancy in electoral politics, Burr had determined to remake himself once more—this time as the leader of a secessionist revolt in the western states. If successful, Burr pointed out to Merry, this plan might mesh with other dreams, cherished by other freebooters, for the conquest of the Floridas and even of Mexico. It would in any case be a grave blow to the newly ascendant Jefferson and to the vast but insecure new American dominions of the Louisiana Purchase. Since British money and vessels would be required, Merry forwarded the plan to London with relish. At a later meeting in late 1805, after Burr had been on a mission of reconnaissance, he reported to Merry that preparations for a rebellion were advancing, and that if Britain did not take advantage of them then the vacuum would be filled by France. Merry seems to have failed to interest London in this proposition. His masters were more preoccupied with the European theater of the war against Napoleon. Burr thereupon turned to Spain, which still resented the loss of the territories.

The fantastic convolutions of the Burr escapade continue to intrigue historians (and novelists, such as Gore Vidal, whose fictionalized account of the affair contains a striking portrait of Jefferson). It is not clear how ambitious Burr really was, or how deeply involved with Spain, or to what extent he suborned mutiny from General James Wilkinson, who commanded American forces in the Southwest. The certainty, however, is that his quixotry (or banditry) held some appeal for the frontier settlers who disliked or distrusted the federal government, and who rather admired the man who had killed Alexander Hamilton, the banker's friend. Jefferson had shown little or no regret at Hamilton's death either, but Burr's was a challenge to his authority that he could not possibly afford to ignore. Quite apart from anything else, as he knew and most other people did not, Lewis and Clark were still out on their mission. The future of the perilously loose, hectically expanded new union was in question. In November

1806, a presidential order was made for the arrest of Aaron Burr on charges of treason.

There followed an interval of alternating drama and farce, with a scramble on the Burr-Wilkinson wing to change allegiance while there was yet time. Rather than wait for this to take effect, Jefferson offered the blunt statement to Congress that Burr's guilt was "placed beyond question." This observation might better have been made after the trial than before it, especially since problems of jurisdiction made it uncertain whether a proper trial could be convened at all. After a comedy of errors involving Burr's arrest, release, and re-arrest in Mississippi—events the proto-defendant milked to the maximum with his customary aplomb—an indictment for treason and conspiracy was presented, in March 1807, at the Fourth Circuit Court in Richmond, Virginia.

Any satisfaction Jefferson might have felt at seeing the arraignment of this clever villain was soon dissipated. The appointed judge in the case was Chief Justice John Marshall, who had so conclusively embarrassed the Republicans in the "XYZ" business and whose political sympathies were widely advertised. No sooner had the trial opened than Marshall threw out the main charge of treason; hard to prove in any event because it required direct testimony about overt acts. This left the court to decide whether Burr had or had not conspired to invade the territory of a friendly power: Mexico. Emboldened, Burr demanded a subpoena requiring the president himself to appear as a witness, and to produce all documents relevant to his defense. This motion was granted by Justice Marshall, and met with indignation from Jefferson, who thus became the first chief executive to plead executive privilege and other immunities. In the result, the demand for Jefferson's own appearance was dropped by the defense, who were rewarded with enough government documentation to make their task an easier one. Faced with layers of legal and political ambiguity, the jurors returned a verdict in the same vein, finding Burr "not proved to be guilty under this indictment by any evidence submitted to us." This, with its echo of the Scottish option of "not proven," did not exactly give Burr a clean bill. But clean bills were probably of less interest to him than his liberty, and he disappeared to Europe for the next five years before returning to New York and resuming the practice of law, as well as of many other of his old reprobate habits.

A lesser man than Thomas Jefferson might have been tempted to demagogy when, in June 1807, even as he was being subpoenaed by Burr's defense team, the British Royal Navy committed a flagrant act of aggression. The frigate USS *Chesapeake*, on its way to the Mediterranean, was stopped by HMS *Leopard*, off the Hampton Roads of the Virginia coast, and ordered to submit to a search. When this order was declined, the *Chesapeake* was raked with several killing broadsides, boarded, and relieved of four crew members. It was the pretext as much as the action itself that kindled a bonfire of rage in American opinion. Great Britain reserved the right to interrupt American maritime traffic, whether naval or civilian, either to "impress" fresh crew members or to retrieve those who had fled

British service. In the preceding year, Jefferson had sent James Monroe and William Pinckney to London to renegotiate the 1795 John Jay treaty as it affected the issue of "impressment." The attempt had been a failure. Bad as this was, the fact remained that only one of the four men seized from the *Chesapeake* had been a "deserter" at all. The other three were American citizens who had originally fled from impressment. Taken to Halifax in Canada, the deserter was hanged and the other three pardoned on condition that they reenlist under the British flag.

So great was the fury in the country at large, and so unanimous was it among both Republicans and Federalists, and so much did it combine long-standing and well-understood grievances with new and inflammatory ones, that Jefferson could easily have secured a declaration of war. He opted, however, to play a longer game. Envoys were dispatched to London to demand redress, while news from Europe was discreetly awaited. Jefferson, having lost most of his illusions about France, was not willing to involve himself in war on either side of the Anglo-French contest. He rather intended to benefit from the balance of that quarrel. This led to a certain conflict in his mind. On the one hand: "I suppose our fate will depend on the successes or reverses of Bonaparte. It is really mortifying that we should be forced to wish success to Bonaparte and to look to his victims for our salvation." But on the other, as he also phrased it, the British were "as tyrannical at sea as [Bonaparte] is on land." His resolution of this conflict was to prepare for war while negotiating for peace. A militia was prepared for an attack on Canada (the old dream again). And the yearning for the South also disclosed itself once more, since war would present another opportunity to remove the Spanish presence once and for all. "Our southern defensive force can take the Floridas, volunteers for a Mexican army will flock to our standard. . . . Probably Cuba would add itself to our confederation." In other words, if it came to it, the great cause of American expansion would not be left to greedy private amateurs like Aaron Burr.

Meanwhile Jefferson's "two-track" policy, forbidding American waters to the British navy while seeking a return of the kidnapped seamen and a settlement of the long-standing impressment issue, was met with frigid contempt by George Canning, the Tory foreign secretary. He regarded Britain as the injured party in the matter, and stood by the "Orders in Council" with which the Crown had claimed the right to interdict any shipping at any time in pursuit of its blockade of Bonaparte. Jefferson thereupon made two decisions that were to stamp his closing years in office. First, in December 1807, he announced that he would not again be a candidate for the presidency. a notable act of renunciation in the circumstances. Second, and later in the same month, he asked Congress to pass the Embargo Act. Both houses granted him convincing majorities. The energy and unity that would have supported a policy of war were channeled, for the first time in modern history, into a program of peaceful sanctions. Henceforward, no American vessels could sail to foreign ports and no foreign vessels could load in American harbors, either. This tactic had been foreshadowed in Jefferson's report, as secretary of state after the Genet fiasco, on the non-belligerent measures available to the United States.

The sacrifice that a nation will endure for a prolonged war is, alas for humanity, often rather more than it will endure for a protracted peace. The high-mindedness and impartiality of Jefferson's policy, which aimed to bring both belligerent powers to their senses (and French raiders had also long preyed on American shipping) was soon dissipated. The high-mindedness suffered from the brute necessity of implementation and enforcement, and the impartiality was tarnished by the perception that the embargo was directed more at Britain than at France. Both objections had some cogency. Albert Gallatin at the Treasury was forced to plug more and more loopholes in the embargo system. Smuggling along the Canadian border—an immensely popular local pastime—had to be discouraged by new rules and new officials. Ship's captains and port authorities, inventive in excuses for unloading or loading certain profitable cargoes, had to be told that there were no exceptions. The libertarian spirit of many Americans was injured, along with their pocketbooks, and the historic image of the oppressive British exciseman was fresh enough to be freely evoked. Paradoxically, perhaps, it was simultaneously alleged that the embargo was anti-French and had been dictated by a secret pact between Jefferson and Bonaparte. Newly unemployed seamen combined with New England Federalists in an agitation that accused Jefferson of stealing bread from the mouths of hardworking Americans. (The metaphor of "bread" was easy to employ, since Jefferson had put himself in the position of a socialist ration-card bureaucrat by deciding to arbitrate the permitted kinds of flour.)

Jefferson's private hope was that the embargo, as well as teaching a lesson to Old Europe, would increase import substitution, encourage production and enterprise in the interior of the country, and generally teach Americans to depend less on others. And indeed, local manufacturing received quite an impetus, especially in Pennsylvania. But overall, at any rate in the short term, farmers began to hoard, sailors and merchants to rebel, and lawyers and customs officers to litigate endlessly or to accept bribes. Jefferson's decision to employ regular army and navy forces to patrol land and sea outlets was, coming on top of all of this, easily interpreted as a panic measure: authoritarianism taking the place of idealism.

There was also some truth to the accusation that the embargo was not impartial. Jefferson admitted that the British were the more vulnerable, being an island nation and having more ships and more colonies. To the end of his days, he believed that greater perseverance would have led to a British capitulation. And it is undoubtedly true that the embargo measures, testifying as they did to the increased strength of America as an economic power, caused great distress and dislocation in British markets. But Napoleon Bonaparte, meanwhile, more than lived up to Jefferson's low opinion of him. He perversely chose to interpret the embargo as effectively pro-British and issued decrees that treated all American ships in European ports as if they were sailing under the British flag. The sole diplomatic consolation was an improvement in relations between the

United States and Napoleon's enemy Russia, which shortly exchanged ambassadors.

In November 1808 Jefferson's preferred candidate, James Madison, won the presidential election with a substantial if reduced Republican majority in the Electoral College. This could have been viewed as a qualified endorsement of the embargo. But the mainspring of the enterprise seemed to have broken, and when Congress had a chance to vote the following March, it replaced the Embargo Act with the much diluted Non-Intercourse Act. There was to be no more American pacific-internationalist involvement in European affairs until the presidency of Woodrow Wilson almost a century later. And the road to the War of 1812 lay wide open.

The signing of the feeble (and feebly named) Non-Intercourse Act was the last act of Thomas Jefferson as president. His second administration had seen little of the dash and initiative and glory that had marked the first one. As he was making ready to leave Washington for the last time, he wrote to Pierre Dupont de Nemours:

> Within a few days I retire to my family, my books and farms; and having gained the harbor myself, I shall look on my friends still buffeting the storm with anxiety indeed, but not with envy. Never did a prisoner released from his chains feel such relief as I shall on shaking off the shackles of power. Nature intended me for the tranquil pursuits of science, by rendering them my supreme delight. But the enormities of

the times in which I have lived, have forced me to take a part in resisting them, and to commit myself on the boisterous ocean of political passion.

This time, Jefferson's self-pity could not be accused of concealing any future ambition. And his recourse to the metaphor of the high seas, commonplace as it was, can in the context be forgiven.

Henry Adams describes America as it was when Jefferson first became president:

According to the census of 1800, the United States of America contained 5,308,483 persons. In the same year, the British Islands contained upwards of fifteen millions; the French Republic, more than twenty-seven millions. Nearly one fifth of the American people were negro slaves; the true political population consisted of four and a half million free whites, or less than one million able-bodied males, on whose shoulders fell the burden of a continent. Even after two centuries of struggle the land was still untamed; forest covered every portion, except here and there a strip of cultivated soil; the minerals lay undisturbed in their rocky beds, and more than two thirds of the people clung to the seaboard within fifty miles of tide-water. . . . Nowhere did eastern settlements touch the western.

And here he describes it as Jefferson's second presidency was winding down:

> March 2, 1807, the Senate adopted a Resolution calling upon the President for a plan of internal improvements. April 4, 1808, Gallatin made an elaborate Report, which sketched a great scheme of public works. Canals were to be cut through Cape Cod, New Jersey, Delaware, and from Norfolk to Albemarle Sound—thus creating an internal water-way nearly the whole length of the coast. Four great Eastern rivers—the Susquehanna, Potomac, James, and Santee, or Savannah—were to be opened to navigation from tide-water to the highest practicable points, and thence to be connected by roads with four corresponding Western rivers—the Allegheny, Monongahela, Kanawha, and Tennessee—wherever permanent navigation could be depended upon . . . A national university was intended to crown a scheme so extensive in its scope that no European monarch, except perhaps the Czar, could have equalled its scale.

Without fully realizing or even quite intending it, Jefferson had helped usher the United States across the span of bridge that led from colonial settlement to continental nationhood. He had also made it (or them) a power that counted in international councils. This had come at some cost to his beau ideal of the agrarian and the communitarian, as well as at a high price for the delicate relationship between the federal Constitution and the states. Unresolved were the questions of involuntary servitude, of the new nation's exact borders, and of the future of non-European tribes. But these matters were henceforth to be approached within the context of an increasingly assertive American modernity.

Chapter Nine

Declining Years

JEFFERSON'S FINAL RETURN to Virginia did not reflect the transition he had supervised, that of the United States into a modern or outward-looking society. To the contrary, he never left the state again, and confined himself chiefly to agriculture and to the production of handcrafted artifacts for the ornament and improvement of his house and farm. However, he continued to play a part in the life of his country. The two subjects that dominated his last years were education and secularism, which proved to be closely related, sometimes in uncomfortable ways. And always, always, and invariably, there remained the stain and shadow of slavery.

The establishment of the University of Virginia was one of only three of his achievements that Jefferson felt worthy of commemoration on his own headstone. The university also culminated, in old age and retirement, the proselytizing interest in general education that he had shown when he was a young Virginia politician. I choose the word *proselytize* deliberately, because it was his plain intention to found a campus that would be independent of all priests and denominations. Perhaps for this reason, he wanted its construction to be partly under his own eye, in the small town of Charlottesville that abutted Monticello, and also desired that its architectural plan be classical, rather than follow the quasi-Gothic model of so many Anglican or Episcopalian colleges. The model would be Palladian. There would be no chairs of divinity or theology. Christianity would be taught as a part of the study of evolution and ethics. Rather than hew to a set curriculum, students would be able to choose their own special subjects. The design of the place—an imposing Pantheon, contrasting with an open lawn and a set of buildings where students and instructors could be close together—was a balance between dignity and intimacy. As far as possible, it was not to be a Virginian university, but the Virginia branch of the universal enlightenment. Only one chair—that of law and government—was reserved for an American scholar. Much of the spacious yet intricate design of this project, with its porticos and columns, can be viewed with pleasure and instruction to this day. But the struggle to have the site completed was as nothing to the struggle, which began in 1819, to have it tenured.

The words *academic* and *bureaucratic* are still near-synonyms in the twenty-first century, and it is scant surprise to learn that Jefferson had to waste endless time in committees and in parochial wrangling. Would his brainchild undercut the local eminence of William and Mary College, his own alma mater? Would there be sufficient funding? Would the place become a center for subversion and delinquency? The last question struck some of the petty-minded with special and particular force. Thomas Cooper, Jefferson's nominee for the professorship of chemistry, would have been a credit to any university, anywhere, at any time. He was a close associate of Dr. Joseph Priestley, the discoverer of oxygen. Priestley, an Englishman, had suffered much for his rationalism, his belief in scientific method, and his sympathy for the American and French revolutions. His laboratory in Birmingham had been smashed by an ugly crowd which had been inflamed by the "Church and King" hysteria, that version of mob rule approved by the British crown and bishops as a weapon against Dissenters. (This hysteria, also directed against Thomas Paine, was approved—in one of his many lapses—by Edmund Burke.) Not only had Priestley been messing about with profane experiments, but he had founded the doctrine known as Unitarianism, by which Jesus of Nazareth was regarded in the light of a mere mortal with ethical opinions, and not as the son of God. Dr. Cooper took the same view, and had also served time in jail under the Sedition Act. His preeminence as a scientist was as nothing when compared to the danger he posed to decency. So, at least, the Virginian Presbyterians claimed. Their leader, John Holt Rice, adopted the additional and typically Pharisaic view that public opinion would not stand for the appointment of an infidel. This was much like the hypocritical argument that Jefferson had confronted, four decades earlier, in the battle over the Virginia Statute on Religious Freedom. To the Presbyterians on this occasion he reacted even more strongly. All sects, he wrote at one point, "dread the advance of science as witches do the approach of daylight; and scowl on the fatal harbinger announcing the subversion of the duperies in which they live." But the Presbyterians were "the most intolerant of all sects, the most tyrannical, and ambitious: ready at the word of the lawgiver, if such a word could be obtained, to put the torch to the pile, and to rekindle in this virgin hemisphere the flames in which their oracle Calvin consumed the poor Servetus."

Merrill Peterson points out with his customary acidity and perspicuity that this outrage on Jefferson's part, marvelously expressed as it was, nonetheless revealed a latent contradiction. There was not supposed to be any opposition between democracy and Enlightenment. The two were supposed to advance hand in hand, as they did against monarchy. Either you trusted "the people" or you did not, and John Holt Rice had appealed to the sovereignty of the majority. At all events, Jefferson agreed to withdraw the appointment of Dr. Cooper. That might have been considered a tactical withdrawal, in view of Jefferson's advanced age in 1819. And so might his weary realization that it was too soon to attract major academic talent from Europe, as he had so long hoped to do. But, in seeking to secure local and political endorsement for the cherished university, he was willing to go one step further and advocate the Charlottesville lawn as a place where future defenders of slavery and states' rights might walk and talk.

The so-called Missouri Compromise of 1820 agreed to the admission of the Missouri territory (itself a child of the Louisiana Purchase) as a slave state. It "balanced" this acquisition by the admission of Maine, formerly a province of Massachusetts, as a free state. In the North, this ungainly and unwieldy bargain set off a colossal agitation against slavery and its extension. Much of the agitation was led by former Tories and Federalists, such as Rufus King, in whom Jefferson recognized historic and personal enemies. He was not above making appeals to the Virginia legislature, in which he argued that Virginia needed its own university in order to prevent the seduction of its brightest sons by northern colleges such as Harvard. Perhaps as many as five hundred of the future leaders of the South, he warned, were up in the Northeast being taught "anti-Missourism" and worse. "This canker is eating at the vitals of our existence, and if not arrested at once will be beyond remedy." The "canker" to which he alluded was not slavery, but the Unionist opposition to it. The idea of a "national university" had been surreptitiously abandoned in favor of a sectional one. At the end, and when it came to it, Jefferson was for "Virginia First."

These and other tactics had their intended effect, however, and the university was chartered and opened by 1825. Jefferson had boldly announced, when the concept was in its formation, "This institution will be based on the illimitable freedom of the human mind. For here we are not afraid to follow truth where it may lead, nor to tolerate any error so long as reason is left free to combat it." This echo of his first inaugural address expressed a courage that was not maintained in the result. Jefferson nervously tried to ensure that the mandatory political and constitutional texts were as far as possible orthodox and Republican.

Perhaps Jefferson succeeded too well in recruiting young swells who yearned to defend the traditional South; at any event the inauguration of the campus was soon followed by the most noisy and depressing kind of student violence. Every sort of spoiled and selfish behavior was on show: finally the old man himself had to ride painfully down the mountain to Charlottesville and it is said that his tears shamed the delinquents.

However much his views, even on education, were inflected and colored by his defensive attitude to slavery, it was in the field of education above all that Jefferson manifested his anticlericalism. The War of 1812 went very badly for the United States, much worse indeed than Jefferson or anyone else might have foreseen. In the early days of the conflict, revisiting an old fantasy, he had prophesied that the American conquest of British Canada would be "only a matter of marching." By the end of the war, the White House had been burned and sacked by Admiral Cockburn as a reprisal for the American torching of what is now Toronto, and the Library of Congress had also gone up in smoke. Writing to Congressman Samuel Harrison Smith of Maryland, Jefferson offered to replenish this awful loss by selling his own library. For this impressive collection of some 6,487 volumes, he asked a payment of $23,999. The bargain was sniffed at by some of the New England Federalists, notably Congressman Cyrus King of Massachusetts, who declared: "It might be inferred, from the character of the man who collected it, and France, where the collection was made, that the library contained irreligious and immoral books, works of the French philosophers, who caused and influenced the volcano of the French Revolution. The bill would put $23,999 into Jefferson's pocket for about 6,000 books, good, bad and indifferent, old, new and worthless, in languages which many cannot read and most ought not."

The bigoted and provincial King might have been even more inflamed if he had studied the system of classification and cataloguing that Jefferson employed. Taking his cue from Francis Bacon's 1605 essay *The Advancement of Learning*, he subdivided books according to the categories of "Memory," "Understanding," and "Imagination," consistently placing the treatment of religion and of ecclesiastical history at a low rung on the ladder of attainment. He had done the same thing when advising his Virginia neighbor and in-law Robert Skipwith on the plan of a "gentleman's library," classifying the Bible at the end of a long list of volumes headed "Ancient History." In the event, Congress overrode Cyrus King and other objectors, and purchased Jefferson's books for the slightly reduced sum of $23,950. The collection and the catalogue formed the core of the Library of Congress until a fire in 1851, which destroyed two-thirds of it and gratified many who thought it had been the devil's work to begin with. Today, the Library of Congress, with its centerpiece in the Jefferson Room, is one of the most splendid public institutions in the world.

To be attacked for impiety was, for Jefferson, no new thing. His friendship with Thomas Paine and his authorship of the Virginia Statute on Religious Freedom had alerted the faithful to the possibility of all kinds of heresy. He did little to appease this kind of feeling, even at election times. He wrote that he cared not a whit whether a neighbor believed in no god or in many gods, since such a private opinion "neither picks my pocket nor breaks my leg." This laconic attitude seemed unpardonably insolent to the believers, and their diatribes were received with coldness in return. Assailed by the Christian fundamentalists during the election of 1800, Jefferson wrote, "The returning good sense of our country threatens abortion to their hopes. They believe that any portion of power confided to me, will be exerted in opposition to their schemes. And they believe rightly; for I have sworn upon the altar of God, eternal hostility against every form of tyranny over the mind of man."

This pledge was made in a private letter to Dr. Benjamin Rush, one of Jefferson's most important and learned colleagues in the American Philosophical Society, so that the mention of the "altar of God" cannot be attributed—like some of Jefferson's more public statements—to any desire to avoid the politically lethal charge of atheism. Rush was a rationalist and materialist but a Deist. He even broke off relations with Thomas Paine—upon whom he had urged the writing of *Common Sense*—when the latter published *The Age of Reason*. Yet he was hardly less determined to purge Christianity of the accretions of superstition and priestcraft that had enveloped it. He more than once pressed Jefferson to clarify his own opinions on the matter. The president was inclined to plead the excuse of other business, but his mind was evidently at work on the subject, and he received additional impetus from the great Dr. Joseph Priestley, whose *History of the Corruptions of Christianity*, composed before he was exiled from England, was one of Jefferson's favorite books. Priestley followed this up by sending Jefferson his treatise *Socrates and Jesus Compared*, and the reading of this brief text in 1804 determined Jefferson upon a larger plan. He resolved to write about the life of Jesus, separating fact from myth and allowing for the distortions of legend and the exaggerations of oral history, and thus to arrive at something like an ethical minimum. Jefferson indeed once wrote that "there is not a young man now living in the U.S. who will not die a Unitarian," and though this may seem like the most preposterously wrong-headed prophecy, there are in fact many millions of educated Americans, Christian and Jewish and of no particular congregation, who now hold views that are not dissimilar.

Such was his veneration for Priestley that Jefferson hoped it would be he who completed the project of renewing and revising the Bible story. But he made a few stabs at the proposal on his own account, pedantically entitled "Syllabus of an estimate of the merit of the Doctrines of Jesus, compared with those of others." In this, he made various statements of the obvious about the Nazarene. "Like Socrates and Epictetus, he wrote nothing himself"; "According to the ordinary fate of those who attempt to enlighten and reform mankind, he fell an early victim to the jealousy and combination of the altar and the throne"; "The doctrines which he really delivered were defective as a whole, and fragments only of what he did deliver have come to us mutilated, misstated, and often unintelligible." This was fairly ordinary stuff. And any larger work was laid aside after Priestley died in 1805. But Dr. Benjamin Rush was to perform one last service. Distressed at the long estrangement between Jefferson and John Adams, he effected a reconciliation between the two men, who gradually took up a correspondence that, as preserved, is one of the great epistolatory treasures of all time. The exchange commenced in 1812. By 1813, the year of Rush's death, Adams, who had become aware of Jefferson's contact with Priestley, was writing to him and urging that he live up to his promise to write about religion. Jefferson replied, saying that the work had already begun, during the few idle hours of his second presidency:

> We must reduce our volume to the simple evangelists, select, even from them, the very words only of Jesus, paring off the amphiboligisms into which they have been led, by forgetting often, or not understanding what had fallen from Him, by giving their own misconceptions as His dicta, and expressing unintelligibly for others what they had not understood themselves. There will be found remaining the most sublime and benevolent code of morals which has ever been offered to man. I have performed this operation for my own use, by cutting verse by verse out of the printed book, and by arranging the matter which is evidently His, and which is as distinguishable as diamonds in a dunghill.

This version, published as *The Philosophy of Jesus* in 1805, was described on its cover as "an abridgement of the New Testament for the use of the Indians, unembarrassed with matters of fact or faith beyond the level of their comprehensions." This certainly matched Jefferson's view that Indians should be protected from Christian missionaries, but some Unitarians have speculated that it also provided him with a respectable cover story for his otherwise profane exercise of cutting up the holy book with a razor blade and throwing away all the superfluous, ridiculous, and devotional parts. (This is an exercise that I have long wanted to repeat in the case of the multivolume hagiography of Jefferson himself, penned so laboriously by Dumas Malone.)

Toward the end of his life, in 1820, Jefferson published a more complete expurgation, in which he excised all mentions of angels, miracles, and the resurrection. As he explained, this was to clarify not just the distinction between Jesus and the interpretation of his disciples, but the distinction between faith and reason:

While this syllabus is meant to place the character of Jesus in its true and high light, as no impostor himself, but a great reformer of the Hebrew code of religion, it is not to be understood that I am with Him in all His doctrines. I am a Materialist; He takes the side of Spiritualism. He preaches the efficacy of repentance towards forgiveness of sin; I require a counterpoise of good works to redeem it. . . . Among the sayings and discourses imputed to Him by His biographers, I find many passages of fine imagination, correct morality and of the most lovely benevolence; and others, again, of so much ignorance, so much absurdity, so much untruth, charlatanism

and imposture as to pronounce it impossible that such contradictions should proceed from the same Being. I separate,
therefore, the gold from the dross; restore to Him the former,
and leave the latter to the stupidity of some, and roguery of
others of His disciples.

Published as a parallel text in Greek, Latin, French, and English,
as *The Life and Morals of Jesus of Nazareth, Extracted Textually from
the Gospels*, this is sometimes known colloquially as "the Jefferson
Bible." In 1904, it became the custom of the United States Senate to
present new members with a copy on the day of their swearing-in.
The Unitarian Universalist Church lays great emphasis on the book,
and though this Church has not succeeded in attracting the majority of American males, as Jefferson predicted, it did many years ago
inaugurate the practice of ordaining women. (This step, with his
general doubt of the fitness of women to hold responsible office, Jefferson would probably not have approved.)

As his days began to wane, Jefferson more than once wrote to
friends that he faced the approaching end without either hope or
fear. This was as much as to say, in the most unmistakable terms, that
he was not a Christian. As to whether he was an atheist, we must reserve judgment if only because of the prudence he was compelled to
observe during his political life. But as he had written to his nephew
Peter Carr as early as 1787, one must not "be frightened from this in-
quiry by any fear of its consequences. If it ends in a belief that there
is no God, you will find incitements to virtue in the comfort and

pleasantness you feel in its exercise, and the love of others which it will procure you."

In May 1824, an itinerant scholar and book peddler named Samuel Whitcomb paid a call at Monticello and found Jefferson himself answering the door. Whitcomb failed to interest the eighty-one-year-old retired president in a copy of Mitford's *History of Greece*, which Jefferson described as containing slurs on the democrats of ancient Athens. Turning hastily to other subjects, Whitcomb found that Jefferson said, of "Negroes" that "he hopes well of their minds but has never seen evidence of genius among them," and of Indians that they "will all dwindle away and be lost in our race by amalgamation." When the inescapable matter of religion was raised, Jefferson became irascible:

> He remarked in reply to me that Paul was the first who had perverted the Doctrines of Christ. I made some remarks and concluded by saying that the Clergy in our Country were investigating these subjects with considerable independence. He dissented and expressed himself warmly in a phrase which I suppose was not English but some other language "The Clergy were all . . ." It was evident to me that he held the Clergy in general in perfect contempt; and that he thought little of Theological investigation. . . .
>
> He is tall and very straight excepting his neck which appears limber and inclined to crook. His hair is long and thin. His eyes light and weak, but somewhat severe. He is more

homely, plain and uninteresting, common and undignified than I was prepared to expect. I should not take him for a generous man. He is more positive, decided and passionate than I had expected. I should think him less of a philosopher than a partisan. His manners are much the most agreeable part of him. They are artifical [sic], he shrugs his shoulders when talking, has much of the Frenchman, is rapid, varying, volatile, eloquent, amusing. I should not think him (did I not know his age) much over 60 or 65 years.

In the same period as he was completing his work of radical biblical revisionism, Jefferson took his last, despairing position on the question of slavery. The Missouri Compromise of 1820, he declared in a letter to one of its authors, John Holmes, had "like a fire bell in the night, awakened and filled me with terror. I considered it at once as the knell of the Union." The old warrior had not lost his gift of phrase. The freeing of slaves in itself, he continued in the same letter, "would not cost me a second thought if, in that way, a general emancipation and *expatriation* [emphasis original] could be effected; and, gradually, and with due sacrifices, I think it might be. But as it is, we have the wolf by the ears, and we can neither hold him, nor safely let him go. Justice is in one scale, and self-preservation in the other." He concluded: "I regret that I am now to die in the belief, that the useless sacrifice of themselves by the generation of 1776, to acquire self-government and happiness to their country, is to be thrown away by the unwise and unworthy passions of their sons, and that my only consolation is to be, that I live not to weep over it." This agony of self-pity, with its rare hint of an elderly tremulousness, also caused Jefferson to express himself in less elegant ways, which hardly indicated that "self-preservation" and "justice" were in equal balance in his mind. "Are our slaves to be presented with freedom and a dagger?" he demanded to know in a letter to Adams. If Congress could override the states on the question of slavery, he said to Albert Gallatin, where would it all end? "All the whites south of the Potomac and Ohio must evacuate their states; and most fortunate those who can do it first." A small but telling episode illuminated his more general coarsening. His old comrade Thaddeus Kosciusko, Polish hero of the American Revolution and victim of the Alien and Sedition Acts, had died in Switzerland in 1817. He named Jefferson as his executor, and left all his money for a fund to purchase the freedom of young black slaves and bestow an education upon them. The sage of Monticello coldly declined to execute his friend's dying wish. He reserved his energies for the idea of "colonization": the euphemism for the expatriation and resettlement of black Americans in Sierra Leone and Liberia.

Placing himself in the ranks of what Virginian conservatives grandly called a Republican revival, and endorsing the work of dogmatic agrarian writers like his friend John Taylor, Jefferson became steadily more pessimistic and choleric. After the election of John Quincy Adams over Andrew Jackson, he wrote a private letter to his old associate William Giles, by now governor of Virginia, in which he revived all his well-worn anti-Federalist tropes. He denounced those who, "having nothing in them of the principles of '76 now look back to a single and splendid government of an aristocracy, founded on banking institutions and monied incorporations under the guise and cloak of their favored branches of manufactures, commerce, and navigation, riding and ruling over the plundered ploughman and beggared yeomanry." Nor was this all. The states should be on guard against the center, he added, and if ever it should come to a choice between "dissolution of our Union . . . or submission to a government without limitation of powers," then the decision must be for secession. So it was the big bad (black) wolf, it turned out, that really had Jefferson by the ears. This letter to Giles was private, and written in 1826 when Jefferson had only a short time to live, but Giles made it public after his death and thus helped create the moral basis for the "states' rights" ideology of John Calhoun.

The historian James Parton claimed roundly in 1874, "If Jefferson was wrong, America is wrong. If America is right, Jefferson was right." This oft-cited declaration is a failure, both as an epigram and as an aphorism. Leave aside the question of whether a man or a nation can be "right." Overlook the absurdity of making the "rightness" of a nation or a country contingent on the rectitude of an individual. Forget that the "rights" which Americans declared are either inalienable or not, and either natural or not, and exist (or do not) independently of any man's will or character. The truth is that America has committed gross wrongs and crimes, as well as upheld great values and principles. It is a society chiefly urban and capitalist, but significantly rural or—as some prefer to say—pastoral. It has an imperial record as well as an isolationist one. It has a secular constitution but a heavily religious and pietistic nature. Jefferson is one of the few figures in our history whose absence simply cannot be imagined: his role in the expansion and definition of the United States is too considerable, even at this distance, to be reduced by the passage of time. But all the above strains and paradoxes, many of which he embodied and personified, would still have been present if he had never been born.

The word *experiment,* as employed to describe the American Revolution in Jefferson's last public letter, has since acquired a different and sinister ring. The defenders of Stalinism used to call their own system "the great socialist experiment" and—like their ostensible Nazi enemies—actually did conduct "experiments" on live human beings. (Not all Communists were always so obtuse. Ho Chi Minh, issuing the declaration of Vietnam's independence in 1945, followed the example of the Seneca Falls conference on the rights of women and phrased his preamble in Jefferson's own words.) The term "experiment," in Jefferson's mouth or from his pen, meant the scientific curiosity of his colleagues in the American Philosophical Society: the humane genius of a Rittenhouse or a Rush or a Barton or a Priestley. The undertaking to be tested was that of self-government. The French Revolution destroyed itself in Jefferson's own lifetime. More modern revolutions have destroyed themselves and others. If the American Revolution, with its secularism, its separation of powers, its Bill of Rights, and its gradual enfranchisement of those excluded or worse at its founding, has often betrayed itself at home and abroad, it nevertheless remains the only revolution that still retains any power to inspire.

Thomas Jefferson had, in the course of a long political life, contained sufficient "multitudes," in Walt Whitman's phrase, to contradict himself with scope and with generosity. He ranged himself on many sides of many questions, from government interference with the press to congressional authority over expenditures, and from the maintenance of permanent armed forces to the persistence in foreign entanglements. In a large number of these cases, his justification for reversal or inconsistency was the higher cause of the growth and strength of the American Republic. In a smaller number, it is not difficult to read the promptings of personal self-interest. At the end, his capitulation to a slave power that he half-abominated was both self-interested and a menace to the survival of the republic. This surrender, by a man of the Enlightenment and a man of truly revolutionary and democratic temperament, is another reminder that history is a tragedy and not a morality tale.